WARNING SHOTS

MEMOIRS OF A SINNER SAVED BY GRACE

By David Q. Tran

Copyright © 2016 by David Q. Tran

Warning Shots
Memoirs of a Sinner Saved by Grace
by David Q. Tran

Printed in the United States of America.

ISBN 9781498484428

All rights reserved solely by the author. The author guarantees all contents are original and do not infringe upon the legal rights of any other person or work. No part of this book may be reproduced in any form without the permission of the author. The views expressed in this book are not necessarily those of the publisher.

Scripture quotations taken from the King James Version (KJV) – *public domain*

www.xulonpress.com

Table of Contents

Prologue ix
Dedication.................................. xi
1. Early Years 13
2. Schools and College 29
3. Military Life 60
4. Prisoner of War and "Reeducation" 99
5. Boat People and Refugee Camps 180
6. New Continent and New Life in Christ ... 202

Epilogue 237

BANG! BANG! Two deafening gunshots reverberated in the quiet jungle. While I was not sure from whence the bursts came, a voice thundered: "Surrender, live. Resist, die!" Turning towards the sound, I saw two soldiers in moss green uniforms with pith helmets standing behind the bushes near the creek, aimed their AK-47s at us; chills ran down my spine.

That was about three in the afternoon, Thursday March 20—the first day of spring, 1975, forty two days before the demise of the Republic of Vietnam; my wife and I were captured by the North Vietnamese Army.

Prologue

My life had been like a small glass ball, thin and fragile, in a watercourse: most of the time it floated in the calm and peaceful stream, occasionally tumbled, submerged, and popped up uncontrollably in roaring white water, splashed around boulders and crags; it was scraped and chipped yet emerged in one piece. Without any merit of my own but entirely as an object of God's mercy, I was spared death time after time, awakened to see my sinfulness beneath a façade of moral decency, and gifted a new life in Christ.

By the urging of my children, here I am to testify the amazing redemptive works of God on me; pray that many readers might also know the Holy Father though Christ Jesus our Lord who upholds my life with boundless grace, compassion, and power.

Our Lord worked miracles and would still do them according to His good pleasure. All the supernatural phenomena and experiences that I witnessed and went through must not be used to validate the doctrines of the Bible, but rather the other way around. Miracles, albeit genuine, cannot lead to true faith, only by the preaching of the person and work of Jesus Christ through the Spirit's quickening power can.

Thanks be to God for our parents, our families, and the innumerable people walked with us on the journey of life. Praise God for the American people who welcomed us into their midst and for reconnecting with some comrades-in-arms to fill in the missing pieces of my jigsaw puzzle.

Dedication

To Anna
My beloved wife
Through her, the Lord God
delivered me from the POW camp,
led me to the saving knowledge of Christ, and
gifted us three children.

May all the glory be to the Father and the Son and the Holy Spirit both now and ever!

Chapter 1.

Early Years

My Mom described her first impression when the midwife showed me to her: "What an ugly boy with a big head!"

I was the third child in a family of five boys. Our family had always been admired as blessed in the Chinese tradition.

My Father

We brothers were born in Vietnam. Our Father Chen-De came to Vietnam in the 1920s at the age of fourteen from Jiangmen of Guangdong.

On legal documents the ages of my parents were a few years younger than the actual ones. It was a common practice to evade the annual body taxes that starting at the age of eighteen, levied by the French colonial authority. Adults in Indochina consisted of Vietnam, Laos, and Cambodia used body tax receipts as proofs of identify.

Our family name is Trần in Vietnamese, Chan in Cantonese, and Chen in Mandarin/Putonghua. Chinese people have a unified writing system but many dialects, therefore our family name carries markedly different pronunciations; depending on the country our kinfolk emigrating to, Chen has been transliterated as Chan, Chin, Ching, Tan or Trần.

Chen was a large family in Guangdong; there was a popular saying "Chen in Guangdong, Li under heaven", i.e. Chen was the commonest family name in Guangdong Province, Li the most populous in China. From the latest census data, Zhang being the biggest family name in China. There was a Chen dynasty in China also a Trần in Vietnam. Besides the largest family of Nguyễn, Trần was also a popular one in Vietnam.

Dad's hometown Jiangmen or The River's Door was not that far from Guangzhou, the provincial seat. Jiangmen was part of a locale collectively called Siyi or the Four Prefectures which consisted of Xinhui, Taishan, Kaiping, and Enping. The Four Prefectures located at the estuary of the Pearl River flowing into the South China Sea. The geographic location facilitated the inhabitants of Siyi ventured out to foreign soils for better lives.

Chinese had moved in large number to Vietnam at the fall of the Ming Dynasty; families of the dignitaries and the military fled the invading Qing Army from the north of the Great Wall. In South Vietnam, a large group of naturalized Chinese consisting of approximately twenty family names whom were collectively recognized by the Vietnamese as *Minh Hương* or Folks of Ming Origin.

Many emigrants sent their savings back home where they yearned to retire and eventually rest in peace; hence Siyi became one of the wealthy enclaves along the eastern seaboard of China.

Language Experience

Since the eighteenth century, many Siyi folks emigrated to Honolulu and San Francisco. Most of the older generation in the U.S. Chinatowns used the Taishan dialect and Dad was able to communicate amiably with those restaurateurs.

Among the Chinese in Saigon and Cholon the dominant tongue was Guangzhou Cantonese, therefore, we understood only very little of the dialogs between Grandma and Dad, or the conversation among Dad's relatives.

Grandmother

Our Grandma was the second wife of a farmer after the first one passed away. Grandma eked out a living as a hired hand in clearing out weeds from the rice paddies. Dad used to assist Grandma in the field and gather firewood from the nearby hills. Once, Dad showed me a bamboo splinter buried beneath his kneecap when he tumbled down the hill to run away from a swarm of hornets; it took him a fortnight to recover from the horrendous swelling by the stings. In the winter, Dad and his younger brother Chen-Cai kept warm with capes converted from jute bags; they had no footwear, therefore suffering minor frostbites on their soles and toes; the villagers called these frostbites "turnips", due to the whitish appearance.

Sojourn in Vietnam

After a stint in Hong Kong as a barber's apprentice, Dad came to Saigon by sea in one of those "big-eyed-cocks"—freighters with eyes painted on the bows—to work in his half-brother Chen-Cheng's dried food shop.

The exciting discovery for Dad was that rice paddies in the fertile Mekong Delta were vastly different from Jiangmen's. The rice in South Vietnam was so vivacious that when the seedlings had been planted there was no breathing room for the weeds; not only that, annually there were three rice harvests. By all means Dad determined to stay, for South Vietnam was the realization of the Chinese proverbial paradise on earth: "the homestead of fish and rice." Alas, our Dad had to leave his earthly belongings behind in Vietnam in 1979!

Family Tree

Grandma gave birth to three sons and Dad was number two; Dad had a half-sister besides the eldest half-brother. Since all the children from the Chinese patriarchal system were enumerated in sequential birth order, therefore, we had First Uncle, Third Aunt, Fourth Uncle, Dad, and Sixth Uncle. Eventually all Dad's siblings went to Vietnam, lived and died there, except him.

My Father's Schooling

Another tale Dad liked to relate was that since the family was so poor, therefore he had gotten only eight months of half-day reading and writing lessons from a village teacher with a handful of pupils. In the dried food shop of First Uncle, when there was that little bit free time, Dad built up his vocabulary by tracing the writings on the sale ledgers and delivery receipts. Through strenuous self-discipline, Dad was able to read the newspapers. As a loving parent, he was willing to provide his children the education that he sorely missed.

Apprenticeship

Dad worked hard in his brother's shop. As an apprentice, he was the first to wake up, wash the teapot and the cups, make tea, and open up shop. He prepared vegetables for the cook, set up the dining table, and washed dishes. At night, he swept the floor and cleaned up after closing.

One night during the usual year-end rush to ship goods to the Mekong Delta, Dad shouldered a loaded bamboo basket going down the long wooden staircase; drowsily, he tumbled headlong down the steps. Fortunately, he suffered no broken bones but scrapes and bruises.

Remarkable Skills

Gradually, Dad mastered the dried food trade. By a glance of the samples, he differentiated the various grades of rice, beans, nuts, preserved vegetables and dried fruits. Dad calculated in his head the costs from Chinese weights into that in kilograms and vice versa. He snapped string and cord grass with bare hand to wrap packages neatly as done by machine. He could sense accurately weights ranged from a few Chinese ounces to tens of kilograms by hand. Once I was concerned about my luggage might exceed the weight limit, so I asked Dad to give an estimate and it turned out exactly as much at the Air Vietnam service counter.

Self-reliance
After acquiring the necessary skills and knowledge, Dad worked on his own as a middleman and went to Cholon—the largest Chinatown in Vietnam, on the west of Saigon.

Dad recounted, somewhat sarcastically, that when Grandma was brought to Vietnam in helping out First Aunt to take care of her ten kids, but the travel cost of Grandma was shared evenly among the four brothers: "one boss" and "three coolies".

When Dad was better off and First Uncle had retired from his business, Dad still treated him graciously as a younger sibling should. At the time of First Uncle's passing, Dad was the executor of Uncle's will.

My Mom
Our Mother Zheng Han-Zhang was born in Vietnam. Her Father Zheng-Ming came from a town called Foshan or Buddha Mountain, a component of Nanhai Prefecture adjoining Guangzhou.

Vietnamese Grandma
Mom's Mother was Vietnamese; therefore we had many Vietnamese relatives. I fondly remembered an old lady selling desserts in Bình Tây Market on the western end of Cholon for her goodies; we were instructed to address her

as Great-grandaunt, by then I did not understand much what she said.

From anthropology, besides the indigenous groups such as Giao Chỉ in the North, Champa in the Central Coast, Montagnard or Degar on the Highlands, Khmer in the Mekong Delta, Vietnamese was Chinese in lineage.

Grandpa

Mom's Dad was a cook before starting his business of paper and thread products; the paper products were flags, accordion lanterns, flower strings and so forth. Grandpa was an inventor, he made a machine that took a few yards of threads from the big spools rolled them into small bundles in the shapes of moon or star, and they were favorite merchandise to the Viet farm ladies for a small price. Grandpa's machine was so unique that a Japanese merchant wanted to buy out Grandpa's invention but he declined, for he was a loyal member of the Kuomintang or the Chinese Nationalist Party. It was a very courageous act during the Japanese occupation of Vietnam.

Mom had a brother Zheng-Lai and sister Zheng-Han-E. Grandma died far away in a Buddhist convent in the Black Virgin Mountain of Tây Ninh Province due to marital conflict with Grandpa. Grandpa married his mistress and had three more daughters. In order to protect her own siblings, Mom got to act like a Big Mama making no concessions to "that mistress."

Uncle Lai

During the 1930s, Chinese schools in Cholon went up only to fourth grade, for further education one had to go to China. Uncle Lai was very intelligent and eager to pursue higher learning, but Grandpa wanted his heir to run the family business.

Hard to imagine that an elementary pupil interested in reading college textbooks, and some of which were in foreign tongue. Uncle Lai had learned that France could not be a world power and studied English on his own. One day, Uncle's secret was unraveled by a Vietnamese client who recognized the book on the counter was in English and the remark was heard; Grandpa was infuriated, for him English was useless there and then.

Grandpa refused Uncle's plea to study in China. Uncle was depressed and became very sick; he murmured all the day long and died a few years later. I guessed that the death of Uncle was partly due to the serious anemia caused by the bleeding hemorrhoids that were prevalent in Mom's family. Uncle Lai passed away in his mid-twenties.

Uncle's Library

When I was in middle school, I flipped through Uncle's books which were brownish in color and some had wormholes as big as peas. Among those books were: general chemistry which used the equal signs in chemical equations, introduction to automotive engineering with illustrations of Model T, beekeeping, and treatise on embroidery in English.

We had a twelve-volume thread-bound Kang Xi Dictionary which might not be part of Uncle's collection, and Mom taught me to repair the binding with similar threads. Kang Xi was the second emperor of the Qing Dynasty; the dictionary was compiled under his auspice. The dictionary compiled the definition and pronunciation of 47,000 individual words. A college student of Chinese literature needed to know 12,000 terms, while 4,000 were sufficient for daily use. Many words in the dictionary were archaic, yet I learned quite a few things from it.

English Dictionaries

Like Uncle Lai I liked books. A book that I read recommended three English dictionaries: the Unabridged Merriam-Webster, Chambers, and Funk & Wagnalls. So, I bought a Chambers and procured the Unabridged with gift money from my parents after passing the Vietnamese high school exam. Besides, I also owned a Shorter Oxford English Dictionary. Currently I had a Funk & Wagnalls, 1954 edition, which I did not find in Vietnam; I picked it up from a yard sale in Connecticut in 1979 for a dollar. To that author I had followed through his recommendations.

Grandpa's House

Before Dad could afford a house, we moved around quite a bit and had stayed in Grandpa's wooden house which was in Xóm Củi or Firewood Village in the Eighth District of Cholon. In the living room hung a portrait of Grandpa in a suit faded to pale brownish hue. Around the fence in the front were red hibiscus, ylang-ylang or eagle talon flowers and vines with purplish black berries. We maneuvered the tender hibiscus leaves onto eyelashes by their gluey sap. The blooming ylang-ylang was very refreshing but sniffing the flowers made me dizzy.

Light Industries

Walking to the canal at the rear of Grandpa's house to see the big logs floating next to the granite dock, we went by a saw mill covered with ankle-deep saw dusts; two workers rhythmically sawing the logs retrieved from the canal into planks. The primitive work scene resurfaced twenty some years later in the Katum "reeducation" camp.

The brick building next door was a textile factory. When it was in operation, a dozen or so big looms produced a noisy cacophony. Thirty years later I saw a similar loom on display in the Natural History Museum in Washington DC. Those machines I saw then were still in use nearly a century after the debut.

Open Sewer
One day, I fell into the open sewer in front of Grandpa's house; Mom splashed on me plenteous amount of water to get rid of the blackish nauseating grime. My elder brothers remembered that I was the only kid ever fell into the sewer.

Huge Fire
On one occasion, we were prepared to flee from a huge fire that was raging on the other side of the Twin Canals. Standing among the nervous crowd, I could see the awesome flames rising upwards while consuming many thatched huts. Dad fetched a cargo truck ready to carry the family and belongings away in case the burning debris dancing in the air got blown over this side of the Canal. Finally, the fire died down and we were spared the run.

There was no modern toilet in that neighborhood; human wastes in big wooden buckets had to be hauled away early in the morning. The thankless job was done by an old man, known as "shit-dumping-Third-Granduncle". Once in a while, I saw the shirtless skinny wrinkled old man, with a curved back, wearing a crumpled felt cap, puffing a hand-rolled cigarette dangled between his lips, trudged along the sidewalk on clogs.

First Traffic Accident
We went to a small Buddhist temple across the street to pick palm nuts and crack them open.

The first traffic accident occurred when I was three or four: I ran from the temple towards home and was hit on the left side by a bike. I was knocked unconscious.

Grandaunt and Uncles

We moved to the row house of a Grandaunt who was a widow with two sons in their thirties. Her sons operated a shop that made slides on glass plates which projected advertisements on the silver screens or print leaflets.

The elder Uncle Zheng-Yan loved photography and frequently took part in photography exhibitions; he showed us film development in his darkroom. Hunting was his other hobby. He rode around town on a scooter.

The younger Uncle Zheng-Wei was homebound due to a spinal problem. He moved around wearing a sarong, taking little steps with stiffened hips and knees. He could not sit down but stand or lie down like a log. He had chest-high tables for dining, board games, and business. It was interesting to watch how he lay down and got out of the elevated bed. The debilitating condition occurred when Uncle Wei was a teenager. He used to hose down the hot cement floor on the terrace then lie down to enjoy a nap on the water-cooled spot. Over time, due to the amount of water used did not do the cooling job well enough, the dissipating heat damaged his spinal cord. Grandaunt sent Uncle to a French physician who put him in a cast. When Grandaunt found that out, in a fury she took Uncle out of the hospital and removed the gypsum cast by chisel and razor blade. The cast was removed but Uncle was stiffened up like that ever since. Very much later, Uncle Wei got into an arranged marriage with a country girl, and the poor lady ran away after the wedding night!

From Uncle Wei we learned to play Chinese checker, and listened to broadcast from a radio with a long tuning needle. The station call of the British Broadcasting Corporation made a vivid impression on me. In my young mind, I wondered about the voices and music coming out of the box.

During this stay, I used the first modern toilet which was the squatting type with a wrought iron water tank high up to the ceiling. People used to splash around the toilet a creamy white liquid with very strong odor which I learned later to be creosote. The toilet papers were thick and coarse also large in size, to be cut in four and strung up with a wire.

It was at Grandaunt's house that we saw an elephant selling Tiger Balm. It was an awesome sight watching the huge animal strolled gently down the road; a man sitting on its back used a gong to announce their presence.

Another Traffic Accident

At that time cousin Mei, one of the three daughters of Sixth Uncle, was helping Mom to take care of me and little brother Ju-Fang. One afternoon, Mei brought the two of us home after a stroll. She carried Fang in her arms and crossed the street, I ran after her and a bicycle hit me on the left, again! Just like the first accident I lost consciousness at impact but suffered no head injury nor broken bones.

One night when I was about eight or nine, woke up in pain and was carried on a maid's back to see a doctor residing a couple blocks away. Whether I got a shot I could not recall but did remember the doctor gave me a tablespoon of milky stuff and its horrible taste of rotten milk lingered for a long time. Up to my high school years, once in a long while, without warning I felt like being struck by a sledge hammer on my left flank where I had been hit twice, the severe pain halted my breathing for a few seconds and then went away.

Heavenly Queen

Several blocks away from Grandaunt's house on Nguyễn Trãi Street situated Mom's alma mater Kun-De, i.e. "feminine virtues", the school as indicated in the name started out as for girls. Next to the school was a shrine of the Heavenly Queen who was worshipped by all Chinese who had emigrated to foreign soils.

By legend, the Heavenly Queen was a virtuous virgin drowned in the sea, and then she appeared during storms at sea to deliver those in distress to safe haven. She was venerated initially as "Lady" and elevated by a Ming emperor to "Heavenly Queen". Coastal inhabitants and Chinese living abroad entrusted their high sea journeys to the Queen, therefore the worship of her was prevalent; whereas in other parts of China one could not find any shrine for her. Each year, the earthen statue from the most prestigious shrine among the many similar ones would be carried around town to spread peace, prosperity, and ward off pestilences; then the statue would be rinsed off and the resulting "holy water" auctioned off as sacred potion which we kids all had taken. The revenues of these shrines from devotees were managed by trustees for charities and religious festivities.

In the shrine adjacent to Mom's alma mater, I was told to go under the half dozen or so altar tables, so that I would grow up smart and filial. The place was dimly lit, upon the altar was a dark statue behind thick embroidered curtains; the air was cold and austere. I hunched my shoulders and tunneled through those tables as fast as possible.

Folk Religions

I grew up with a syncretism of ancestor worship, Confucianism, Taoism, Buddhism, animism, and Spiritism. As most Chinese we had idols in and around our home. On the family altar there was a ubiquitous plaque honoring the ancestors flanked by the couplet:

Forefathers planted the honest fields
Offsprings plow the blessed furrows

Traditionally we worshiped the deceased up to five generations. In front of the joss stick urn displayed a small cardboard wrapped in red paper, with the names of five consecutive male heads of previous generations; their dates of birth and death in lunar calendar. The names of our ancestors recorded were used uniquely for their nuptials. For Chinese of old, a male had many names: a name at birth, for school, at wedding, for literary works, even at death.

We were told that the complete genealogy dating from the first Chen settled in Jiangmen had been kept in the family shrine. A few years ago, my fifth brother Ju-Xiang went to visit our ancestral land; the shrine was no more, a thoroughfare bearing the village's name was the only vestige.

On the altar, the ancestral plaque was flanked by a statue of the Goddess of Mercy or Guan Shi Yin—one who observes the pleading sounds of mankind. On the other side was a drawing of three people: seated was the red-faced, long-bearded Guan-Yu or Guan-Gong, namely Archduke Guan; standing on the left the white-faced Guan-Ping his nephew was holding a big seal, and on the right the black-faced Zhou-Cang the armor-bearer holding a long saber. Guan-Gong was of the Han period, Third Century A.D., depicted in novels as a loyal general, the embodiment of righteousness; henceforth his presence could repel evil spirits. Statues of Guan-Gong were enshrined in the prominent spots in nearly all the Chinese restaurants and groceries.

On the base of our altar was a plaque for a deity with a double title and double duty in charge of the security of the house as well as the family's financial success.

In the kitchen we had a grotto for the kitchen god who was an emissary from heaven to keep an eye on the daily affairs of the family and report to the Jade Emperor at the year's end. One week before the New Year, we sent the kitchen god heavenwards by providing him sugarcane as ladder and offered him glutinous balls in syrup, so that he could not open his mouth to report bad things. Then he came back on New Year's Eve. The Vietnamese had kept a tradition, which was not practiced by the Chinese, of presenting a humorous kitchen god's report as part of the New Year celebration.

On the front we had two additional guardians of the home, high up was the heavenly magistrate and on the ground an earthly one. Twice a day, morning and evening, someone in the family, I occasionally, put joss sticks in the urns. There was more reinforcement on the lintel: an octagonal mirror with the eight Yijing trigrams hung on a trident to keep all the evil spirits and spells at bay.

Some families had special places to offer joss sticks by the toilet's door and under bed. The spirit at the bathroom or bedroom was known as the Third Aunt of the Toilet or Third Aunt of the Headboard. If a family member got sick, joss sticks and paper money must be offered to appease her.

Peculiarly, on a relative's altar, there was a big plaque that I saw only once in my lifetime, written were three words "Revere as present" (after I was saved it struck me as the "unknown god" in Acts 17:23). Some families even had a spot for the Monkey King from the Chinese classic Odyssey of the Monkey.

Our family did not go all the way like some others in consulting fortune-tellers or mediums for illness and problems.

Money First

Money was important but Chinese had blatantly put money in the forefront of daily living; partly due to our long history of suffering therefore money assumed to be the all-powerful protector. Kids got lishi or lucky money beneficial to business, in small red envelops, on all festive occasions of New Year, birthday, wedding and so on. Even in funerals, lishis wrapped in white were handed to mourners to negate the ills of death.

On lunar New Year's Eve, all would stay up to send off the old year and ring in the lucky new. After midnight many young people ran around the city, stopped by every door that was open, to deliver pieces of red paper with the words "god of fortune" and get small tips in return. We got at least half a dozen of these red slips in the first hour of the New Year. The New Year greeting of "gong xi fa cai" wishing each other lots of money.

Many Chinese consulted fortunetellers in order to pinpoint a propitious date and hour for opening a business, moving to a new location, or burying the dead. We hired feng shui experts to get an advantageous orientation of the desk, the house, shop, even burial site. A lucky house number or a license plate with special number was to facilitate raking in more moneys. In the same vein, the display of a big-bellied Amida Buddha or the drawing/figurine of a deer which was homophonous to fortunes would bring in much dough.

From New Year's Eve to the fifteenth day of the New Year was a period to visit temples and shrines, to check out the fortune of the coming year from the resident fortune-tellers. We went with Mom on New Year's Eve, to worship the Heavenly Queen or Guan-Gong and brought home some joss sticks for good luck, peace, and happiness. The shrines were jam-packed and filled with smokes from the joss sticks; the workers were busy pulling out the joss sticks people just offered up and douse them in water buckets. It was a fun-filled occasion for young men to watch pretty girls in new clothes, also good time for pickpockets.

Haunted Life
We lived in a world filled with ghosts. When we boys came back from the movies or opera house late at night and needed to urinate at a lamp post or against a wall, we were to say "Please step aside, let me pee." otherwise we could offend some spirits.

During the seventh month of the lunar calendar, the Month of Ghosts, people burned large quantity of paper money and offered food to the ghosts that had no families.

Fortune-telling, palm-reading, Chinese Ouija board and séances were part of life. All important events, from cradle to grave, required consultation of the four astrological times of birth: year, month, day and hour. Each of the Chinese zodiacs designated in two words, therefore everybody's fortune was hinged on the "eight words". I was horrified to see horoscope and feng shui were so prevalent in the "enlightened" West.

Chapter 2.

School Years and College

After a couple more moves Dad bought his first home. The house was in an alley adjoining to an elementary school from which most of us graduated.

Battle of Điện Biên Phủ
   Around the period of moving from Grandaunt to our first house I heard of the battle of Điện Biên Phủ among the adults. Would ever a young kid imagine that a battle in 1954 affected several countries and millions of lives including his own two decades later?

Poor Health
   I was the frail child in the family and did not begin to walk until I was two. I went to see doctors and herbalists quite frequently. I got used to take the bitter Chinese medicine in liquid, pill, or powder form. I was praised by the doctors and nurses who gave me injections for I never cry, my leg only jerked slightly when the needle hit my butt. On one occasion, I got a big boil on my neck, the doctor used a lancet sanitized on open flame to drain it, a profusion of pus gushed out and I was calm the whole time.

I inherited hemorrhoids from Mom and had gone through seven operations, the first time at the age of twelve. I had high blood pressure at late teen years and glaucoma since mid-thirties, thank God that they were under control through medication and surgeries. There was a Chinese saying: Habitually sick men become physicians. In my life I had been involved in medicine or related matters. When I was captured, the captors called me Doc; shortly before the release from the "reeducation" camp, I was appointed as one of the four "camp doctors" for a month.

Compulsory Naturalization

I was influenced quite a bit by my eldest brother Ju-Hua who was very opinionated though usually on the wrong side of the arguments. Affected by his strong opinion on the compulsory naturalization of Chinese during President Diệm's rule, I blurted out in my fourth grade class "Let's go out and demonstrate!" It was overheard by the homeroom teacher who sternly told me to shut up.

On the issue of naturalization, we Chinese in South Vietnam were critical on the two Chinese regimes on either side of the Taiwan Strait for inaction on our behalf. In the past, Chinese overseas contributed in finance and manpower to topple the Qing Dynasty and contributed to Kuomintang. We split into two camps after the recent establishment of the People's Republic of China, unless one was too extreme in one political view or the other, we just lived and let live. We deemed ourselves "superior" to the local people, history-wise and culture-wise, and would not like to be the citizenry of an "inferior" nation. None of the two Chinas would bring us back and we had no means to repatriate but accept what had been decreed by the Vietnamese government, with resentment. We refused to identify with the Vietnamese in the national life most conspicuously in military service. The sad thing was that we were so inconsistent: we left our miserable homeland for better life yet held on to the glorious past than to be citizens of the country that accepted us.

Our family did plan to go to Taiwan, the Republic of China, Mom and we boys would leave first and Dad stayed to provide financial supports. Taiwan sent a few military aircrafts to bring back some and then the airlift operation came to a halt.

One evening, three children of First Uncle in their teens came to bid farewell before heading to Mainland China. Our cousins became engineer, pediatrician, and teacher in China. Eventually, they came and stayed in the States.

Sino-Vietnamese Connection

Vietnamese and Chinese had been close-knit for centuries. Linguistically, some Vietnamese words retained the ancient Han tones. Ethnically, Vietnamese were Chinese migrated from Guangdong since the Han Dynasty; they conquered the indigenous people and established the Viet nation. Among the neighboring countries of China, Vietnam was the only one ruled by the Chinese for more than a thousand years.

In Cholon, pretty much a self-contained Chinese society, we used our limited Vietnamese to do business with the Vietnamese, on the other hand many Vietnamese could speak Cantonese. We read Chinese dailies and evening news; imported books, magazines and novels from Hong Kong and Taiwan; watched Chinese movies, Cantonese operas; listened to Chinese broadcasts; ate Chinese food, dim sum, and studied in Chinese schools.

Once the naturalization went into effect, the compulsory Vietnamese education also took place. The Vietnamese educational system replicated that of the French, classes were half-day, twenty hours per week. To comply with the requirement, our improvisation worked out well. Chinese schools put in thirty nine periods per week: seven periods each day plus four on Saturday morning. As physical education and music were counted as neutral, all we needed was to teach eighteen hours of Vietnamese, that was how we managed to continue Chinese instruction. The Vietnamese government by then was much more lenient than all the other countries in Southeast Asia where Chinese education were banned.

Elementary School

The grade school I attended was named Nanhai or South Sea, the hometown of our maternal Grandpa. Our alley adjoined to the school, before a concrete partition was raised, we could view from our kitchen the multipurpose hall where the principal and some teachers stayed after school to play Cantonese music. The sounds of collective reading and singing from the school filled the alley during school days.

The Neighborhood

The alley consisted of fourteen houses in two opposite rows. The houses were small, only three meters wide and eight meters long.

House number one had no number plate and the door had been sealed with bricks for it was annexed to a business on the major street. It had a big side entrance from which we saw BMW motorcycles were taken out of cartons and stored inside.

Houses number two and four were built as a bakery which brick oven took up nearly half of the space. Workers fired up the oven with woods for hours, after removing the burnt debris, they cleaned up the oven floor with water-soaked jute bags on long wooden rakes. The workers improvised a tin can, utilizing acetylene gas, as search light to illuminate the pitch-dark interior of the oven. After the cleaning, prepared doughs were put in the oven, mostly for baguettes and croissants. When the breads were done, the fresh aroma spread throughout the alley. Occasionally, we kids went to watch the workers mixing flour in a big wooden trough, or help cut up the unsold baguettes for Melba toasts.

House number three was occupied by the Zhou family with four kids. Sat by the door, Mrs. Zhou's sister was always busy making toothbrushes. She used fishing line to secure the pig bristles on the brush made from animal bone; she gathered a small bundle of bristles from a bamboo tray, flushed and pulled them tightly into the brush; finally, she used a foot-driven grinder to pare the bristles into the standard crescent shape.

House number five probably was the poorest in the alley. Mr. Gu made red ink for teachers to grade Chinese calligraphy homework, and sold baguettes. Mrs. Gu was a survivor of small pox with her telltale pockmarked face. Their two daughters went to evening school for the disadvantageous working class.

House number six resided another Chen family whose head was a widowed dressmaker. Her son played basketball in the middle school and frequently coughed up blood allegedly by injuries suffered in the ballgame, or an unconfirmed case of tuberculosis? Lived there also was Mrs. Chen's brother who worked in the Đại Thế Giới or Grand World Casino owned by a warlord.

Number seven's housewife was a businessman's concubine. Her young brother was in my fourth grade class when he died from meningitis. People said that he died because the hospital took all his blood.

House number eight used to be a candy factory where female workers got paid by the weight of candies they wrapped. We seldom went there to get freebies, for we had better ones at home. After the molten syrup coming out in strips through a hand-roller and separated into candy drops, the workers wrapped them in cellophane and put in bamboo buckets. The workplace was equipped with many small swiveling fans to cool down the sweatshop. One day, a male worker poured the molten syrup from a big wok onto his abdomen, and he was hurt seriously. He was put lying on a work bench and moaned in pain very loudly. The owner was informed by phone then a big jar of tangerine pulp was brought in and spread on the man's wound; gradually the moaning decreased and stopped. Months later the worker came back to visit, his entire abdomen was pinkish with ugly thick scars. Eventually, the candy factory shut down and the house was occupied by a family came from Hải Phòng after the Geneva Accords of 1954. I observed closely their nanny, a traditional North Vietnamese woman, with black teeth which shiny hue was dark purple not charcoal black as I had imagined.

House number nine lived a Li family with frequent strives between two wives. The second wife spit her blood in the alley to prove how she suffered from the lack of care from the husband (another case of tuberculosis). The man also worked for the casino. On a weekday afternoon during school hours fire started from the sugarcane residues drying on the terrace and the fire was put out in time, otherwise the alley would have been devastated. One of the twin daughters of the second wife had parallel rows of teeth in her mouth. It was grotesque!

House number ten resided a Ye family, the housewife was also a seamstress. Her older sister lived in house seven; her younger sister was a taxi dancer, so Mrs. Ye made modern dresses for the dancers. During a prolonged period of the husband's unemployment, we heard quarrels all the time. They had two girls and two boys. This house added two more stories after we moved away.

House number eleven was the Zhu's, a trader of Chinese herbs; his wife was formerly a taxi dancer. We used to gather around their radio to hear kung fu tales from Hong Kong for it had better reception. After the Zhu's departure, a Ding family operating a French cuisine restaurant moved in. The French restaurants and Cantonese coffee shops in Saigon-Cholon

School Years and College

were primarily operated by Hainan people. Hainan folks used to keep the newborns lying on their backs therefore they grew up with heads that were quite flat. One of the two boys' head was so flat that I liked to touch for fun.

Our home was number twelve. Behind the wooden panel partition of the living room was our bedroom which also served as the dining room; there were two bunk beds besides our parents' bed. The extension at the rear contained the kitchen, patio, toilet/bath and reservoir. A metal ladder led to the terrace for hanging laundry.

Our house was facing west; hence nearly all the houses on the same side had canvas awnings. We would prop up the awning on two long poles at noon and took it down before sunset or when it was stormy.

Like all the other houses, ours had an attic with a skylight, during the summer it felt like an oven up there and it was Grandma's sleeping quarters. Occasionally, a bookkeeper from Dad's partnership came to work in the attic and set a desk fan on full power. He had very good handwriting and liked to draw us pictures with his fountain pen. He got a deep dimple as the result of a molar extraction.

House thirteen had once been the residence of a businessman's mistress, then two Zhong families from Hải Phòng moved in consecutively. The first Zhong couple both wore eyeglasses; they stayed a few years then moved to the neighboring street.

The young brother of Mr. Zhong befriended me and taught me how to play harmonica, I bought a Horner harmonica and an instruction manual, and played harmonica for the next ten years. He had an 8mm movie projector and showed me all the silent movies of Charlie Chaplin and French puppets in his collection. Once he brought me to see a Chaplin movie and we sat on the front row. I was bothered by the closeness to the silver screen and threw up, so we had to leave. He was

Warning Shots

twenty some years my senior, there were no abuses in our relationship at all.

The second Zhong family had seven kids, the biggest family in the alley. The father drove a Lambretta scooter. Once he was rushed to the hospital after vomiting a lot of blood due to peptic ulcer; the congealed blood like dark red Jell-O splattered all over the alley as he was held up by two men to board a taxi at the alley's entrance. He survived and recovered.

House number fourteen resided another Li family. The father owned a business selling imported fruits, cookies, liquors, etc. and was Dad's client. My parents were so eager to have a daughter so they "adopted" the Li's youngest as daughter.

Once day, we brothers played badminton in the alley, in the heat of the game, grandma Li who was squeezing by was hit on the head by a racket. Immediately, a purplish lump was formed on the forehead, she moaned out loud and sat down on the ground; her maid used the sole of a slipper to rub on the lump, trusting the uncured rubber of the sole could ameliorate the pain and swelling. This incident brought profuse apologies from our parents. After that, no more badminton games in the alley for us.

Behind the wall by the entrance of the alley was a tiny shrine for the guardian of the alley. Although it was in ill repair, but got its fair share of joss sticks from all the neighbors.

On the street across from our alley, there was an opium shop among the stores and homes; we were told not to go near it. In the shop, people reclined on a big common wooden bed to smoke opium.

Deaths in the Family

Grandma passed away at home in her mid-seventies when I was seven years old. Due to the hot climate Grandma was buried the next day while our Father was in Đà-Nẵng and Huế on a business trip and not able to fly home for the funeral. Papa came home a day after the funeral and was very sad for missing to see Grandma's face for the last time. In lieu of Dad, Sixth Uncle was the filial representative to lead Grandma's funeral.

The occasion left me a horrified memory of seeing the corpse of Grandma lying in the living room waiting for the coffin. The mourning, the noisy tedious religious ceremony with lots of paper money burning, the funeral procession and the succeeding seven weekly ceremonies made me sobbed a lot. Separation from Grandma was heart-breaking even for a carefree boy.

A year or so later, instead of the arrival of a daughter whom my parents were eagerly expecting, our sister was born dead, asphyxiated by the umbilical cord. I remembered seeing Mom sat sorrowfully at her meals served by a maternity aide hired for the occasion.

Sounds of War

On one afternoon, we had haircuts in front of our home from an itinerant barber and heard sporadic yet distant gunfire. The barber hurriedly finished his job and went home. All the doors in the alley were shut. Mom told us to stay underneath the big wooden bed then she went to the nearby grocer to get some salted eggs and dried fish, the survival food of wartime. The uncle from house number six went out to scout for information and came back to announce that it was the end of the conflict between President Diệm and the warlord Lê văn Viễn.

After the ouster of the warlord, the opium dens, the two Casinos along with the daily lotto and legalized prostitution were outlawed.

The School Settings

The school hours were from eight to noon, after lunch break classes resumed at two thirty and ended at five thirty.

Most pupils walked home for lunch and took a nap. Some pupils lived further away stayed in school for lunch and took siesta in the classrooms. We never drink directly from the tap, the school provided boiled water in large urns and students brought their own collapsible plastic cups. We had no nurses in the school but there was a sickroom beneath the staircase of the main building.

From first to third grade, our singings were accompanied by pump organs. There was a piano in the multipurpose hall which also served as assembly hall, teachers' offices, fourth to sixth grades' music class, singing contests, and graduation exams. The school had a concrete basketball court but no spectator stand, it was used for assembly when the weather permitting. Between classes we ran around in the hallways, jumped rope, or played shuttlecock in the basketball court.

Later on, the school expanded upwards, a terrace on the fourth story level could hold the entire student body for movies after dark. We watched "The Wizard of Oz" projected on large white wooden panes. On one occasion, the whole school went up to the terrace to watch an international airshow. Outside the assembly hall, there was a ping-pong table next to a wall of white marble panels carved with Chinese writings.

The capacity of our classrooms ranged from fifty to eighty pupils. Some teachers had not even been to high school but were capable to provide good instruction. They had to speak loudly to the large classes and used rattan rods as blackboard pointers. We had Chinese calligraphy homework daily in addition to other class assignments.

When school rules were broken or homework not done, students were disciplined by a few strikes of rattan rods on the palm or buttock, these rods were standard disciplinary instruments at homes too. I remembered how it felt like to be whipped by these rods. What a contrast with the modern school system which had been deprived of authority and could not keep up with thirty-student classes, got rid of corporeal punishment deemed inhumane and damaging to self-esteem.

From fourth grade on, we had scout instructions on salutation, parade, tying knots, etc. Chinese scouts saluted with three fingers representing the Confucian virtues of wisdom, goodness, and bravery. Pupils in scout uniforms took turn to serve as guards at designated stations, maintain order during breaks. Some served as crossing guards, under supervision of teachers, for school dismissal at noon and evening.

Our grade school uniforms were white short-sleeve shirts with white khaki shorts for boys and back skirts for girls. On the left breast of our shirts we pinned a triangular emblem of the school.

At the last day of the school year, pupils were given prizes, in most cases 100-page notebooks, for perfect attendance, top three pupils of the class, and contest winners in various subjects and so on. After the closing ceremony one could notice those "good" pupils carrying stacks of new notebooks home.

Our school celebrated the Chinese Children's Day on April 4, "four-four" sounded like teeny in Cantonese. It was an exciting day when all classes were cancelled; pupils went to the assembly hall to draw tickets and bring home goodies bags linked to the numbers. Any number ending in four was more special and the biggest prize went to the number forty four.

A few families requested an initiation ceremony for their heirs. I saw our neighbor's boy, wearing traditional Chinese clothes in white linen, ushered into the school library by a paper lantern to pay homage to a full-size portrait of Confucius—the revered teacher of China, with candles and joss sticks.

Learning Vietnamese

When the Vietnamese curriculum was put in place, my parents hired a female tutor to teach us Vietnamese, and later on English. This lady was good in Vietnamese, English, and French. Through her tutoring, my elder brothers and I enjoyed an edge over our peers. My pronunciation of Vietnamese was good; therefore I was to sit at the front row of the class, from third to fifth grades. When the Education Ministry's inspectors came, we front row pupils could showcase the success of Vietnamese education in the school.

One thing I missed from our tutor was that I did not learn French from her; otherwise I could be fluent in French too. When I tried to learn French in my late teen years, mastering French grammar was too time-consuming so I dropped out.

To me, Vietnamese must be the easiest language to read; once you learned the alphabets and the five intonations you could pronounce every word within a month.

In one way, the colonization of Vietnam by the French brought along educational benefits to the Vietnamese. Before the invention of the Westernized alphabets, Vietnam adopted the Chinese writing and contrived a system called *Chữ Nôm* or Nôm Characters which appended additional strokes to Chinese scripts to indicate their distinctive Vietnamese sounds. Such a cumbersome system limited its usage to only the privileged class. The Vietnamese alphabets were developed by the Portuguese Roman Catholic missionaries and systematized by Alexandre de Rhodes, a French Jesuit, in the Seventeenth Century. These alphabets contributed to the advantage of Vietnamese people in learning European tongues over the other Orientals. It took me more than five years to attain to a working knowledge of the Viet language, because I did not really need to practice it.

My Reading Materials

In Cholon more than a handful of Chinese newspapers were published daily and distributed all over South Vietnam; there were morning, evening, and afternoon news. We used to have two newspapers through home delivery.

Besides the front page of news and editorials, there were many sections in the papers, such as romance, mystery, sci-fi, foretune-telling and feng shui, history, poetry, cuisine, health and folk medicine. Among the novels section, the most popular were kung fu and romance. Two favorite novel writers were Jin-Rong (Kim Dung) and Qing-Rao (Quỳnh Giao). Their voluminous fictions printed daily in segments, and appeared in Vietnamese papers the day after. When I was in the military, some physicians seeing that I picked up my Chinese papers every evening, they asked me to orally translate the kung fu novel of Kim Dung for them.

Some tidbits in a hunting column were very interesting. The writer suspected that his hunting partner had kept a secret about tiger to himself. One day they encountered a tiger in the jungle; the partner tried to shoot the tiger but could not due to some troubles with the trigger mechanism, so he told the author to do it. The author seeing that they were not in immediate danger, therefore he waited to see how his partner would react. When the tiger was approaching, the partner pointed the barrel of his rifle to the tiger and drew a big circle, the tiger halted and skipped back. The partner cursed the writer and kept pushing the tiger back with the same circular movement. Finally, he cleared his trigger and fired at the tiger which was wounded and ran away. Afterwards, there was a quarrel on the author's nonresponse in the crisis; but they were reconciled when the author exposed his partner's selfishness in not to share that lifesaving trick.

Through this incident, the author solved a puzzle he held on for a long time: why a famous Buddhist temple in Guangdong, situated in the forest, used whitewash to draw many big circles around the temple. It turned out that by doing so no tiger would come near the temple.

To prove the truthfulness of the story, we brothers tried it out on our feline at home. Each time we drew a big circle around the head of the cat from a distance, either with our arms or a stick, it arched its back and jumped rearwards.

That column author also described that once he went to see a friend and was approached by two ferocious German shepherds, but they suddenly recoiled and ran away with tails between their hind legs. Eventually he realized that he had a few whiskers from a tiger in the wallet; just the scent of the king of the jungle was enough to scare away the big dogs.

Besides the Chinese newspaper subscriptions, Dad subscribed several magazines and juvenile periodicals from Hong Kong. From all these materials, with my love of reading I gained more diverse knowledge than most of my peers. At fifth grade I was the runner-up in the school's general knowledge contest and was the champion a year later.

I was born with a pretty good voice and had always been one of the favorite singers in class. I attended every singing contest in grade school, although I did not win any prize. Once in fourth grade, the music teacher picked me out and gave me a quick lesson so that I would conduct the school chorus in the citywide tournament; for some reason, she did it herself eventually.

For many families, education had been a privilege. A few of my classmates were much older than me, especially girls; either because they started out late or the parents let the boys attend school first. A fifth grade classmate quit school midway to get married.

Gospel Publications

My first encounter with biblical literature in Chinese was through the Adventists who distributed individual copies of the Four Gospels as well as their flagship magazine Signs of the Time. The magazine was interesting reading but the Gospels were boring to me.

Sanitation and Hygiene

I was prone to motion sickness in my youth. When I was fourteen, I was troubled by dizziness so much that a French doctor diagnosed me with intestinal parasites. After taking some medicine and castor oil in syrup as laxative, two motionless roundworms came out in the excrement. They looked like chubby earthworms about eight inches long. Half of the pinkish bodies of the worms were much darker in tint, probably due to the medication that knocked them out. On the follow-up visit, the doctor questioned why we did not bring the worms in for verification. I was greatly relieved from dizziness from then on.

The water pipes in the city laid down by the French were so old that running water was red in color due to tiny flakes of rust. People put water in cisterns and put alum or quicklime to settle the rust or set up a simple filtering system. We used a big urn consisted of layers of sand, pebble, charcoal and coconut coir. When the sand and pebbles changed color to dark red, we replaced them with new ones.

Later on, when the Americans came and drilled many deep wells, like most city dwellers we purchased the potable water from water trucks.

Some businesses imported a ceramic water filter urn from Japan and it became a common fixture in many homes and businesses.

Bedbugs were everywhere, even in seats of theaters and cinemas. One's butt and legs could get red welts after watching a show. In our home, we had mosquito nets for all the beds, and we sprayed insecticide from hand pumps around the house after dark as a daily routine or sometimes we lit up the mosquito coils. The edges of our mosquito nets were weighed down with bed bug rods—big rods four to five feet in length, with holes drilled on four sides served as hideouts for bed bugs. In a fortnight or so, we took the rods out and drop them repeatedly on the concrete. Lo and behold, bedbugs and whitish eggs came out; it was time for us competing to smudge the bedbugs with clogs or flip flops; some of them were bulging with blood. Afterwards, we poured boiling water on the rods then dried them under the sun. Sometimes we put insecticide powder into the holes of the rods.

Cockroaches were abounding especially in the kitchen area where firewood was stored. I got a very sensitive tongue, sometimes I tasted the awful scent of roaches left behind on dishes they crawled over but others could not, and I was chided as too imaginative. The most powerful weapon against these Oriental or German roaches was the insecticide from the spray cans, you aimed at the roach and pressed the knob immediately the roach turned upside down jerked its legs uncontrollably and died. One of the most frightful folk remedies for treating asthma was mashed cockroaches and hot water, Mom saw Grandma did that in trying to ameliorate her asthma attack.

Talking about health maintenance, routinely herbal teas were served at home; various meat and vegetable dishes were frequently promoted for good health. Rubbing medicated oil and coining were applied to treat headache or common cold.

Massage and cupping services were available from itinerant masseurs on bicycles; they shook a clip of flattened soda bottle caps as their service signal. When people played mahjong through the weekends, they employed masseurs to help stay active through the games.

We had herbalists who also treated broken bones, dislocated shoulders, or sprained ankles with muscle manipulation in conjunction with medicated alcohol rubs. A maid of ours slipped and had a hip joint dislocated; an herbalist made the house call and maneuvered her leg back into the pelvic socket. The procedure did help, but from then on she walked with a limp.

School Years and College

Once in a while, we got candy treat purchased from a hawker on bike: the pink six-petal shaped hard candy containing santonin. It was the popular anthelmintic for kids.

There were no lawns or gardens for most homes in the city, but our surroundings were quite rustic. We saw sewage rats, heard cocks crowing in the neighborhood, dug up earthworms, caught crickets and dragonflies, even raised chicks and ducklings in the alley.

Vaccinations

In my generation all newborns had been vaccinated for small pox; for boys they were done on the legs and the inner thighs for girls. When we wore shorts the two or three big marks of vaccination were clearly seen. School children got small pox vaccine boosters annually; in most schools they were carried out by nurses from the local hospitals. The nurses scratched firmly on our skin with a stylus, then applied the gluey white paste. When there was an outbreak of cholera or influenza, we also had injections in schools. Once in a while, there was news of fatalities from meningitis or bubonic plaque.

Daily Meals

For breakfast, we frequently went to the street corners where food vendors gathered. We chose from sticky rice, hominy, baguette, Cantonese deep-fried dough and so forth. The costs of breakfasts ranged from half to two piasters. At one period of time before the establishment of the Bank of Vietnam, people split the one piaster bill into two fifty-cent pieces, for the sake of convenience. The kind of glutinous rice that I liked was purplish in color; the green or reddish orange ones got their colors from food dyes. The rice and hominy were served on banana leaves with scoops out of palm fronds. The toppings for the glutinous rice were mung bean paste and roasted sesame seeds, for the hominy, shredded coconut and roasted sesame seeds.

After school, we had home-cooked sweet soups with mung bean, red bean, or lotus seed; or baked buns of red bean paste, shredded coconut etc., from a vendor on bike.

On Sundays, we ordered Cantonese noodle soups or wontons from a nearby noodle shop which made home delivery. Quite frequently, the family went out to dim sums; after all the roasted pork buns and chicken feet, our meals concluded with a big plate of deep-fried noodles Cantonese style. There was a popular saying: "Born in Suzhou, dine in Guangzhou, clothe in Hangzhou, and die in Liuzhou" respectively those Chinese cities were famous for good look or good food or good silk or good coffin.

City life was very noisy, food sellers or journeymen hawked their merchandises from sunrise to midnight. Each vendor had his trademark announcement. A cloth dyer used a swinging hand drum, another one made impact noise with his huge wooden clogs. Tinkers and cutlery sharpeners used a rattling string of tins, while a candy man hitting his thick cutter with an iron hook. Ice cream sellers always used bells, and a guy selling shredded green papaya with beef jerky opened and shut his big scissors. After nightfall, only food vendors came out, with lighting either of storm lanterns or acetylene lights, they sold sweet soups, or steamed sugarcanes, or baluts. Sometimes one needed not the trademark hawking for the peculiar aromas had already announced the arrival.

It was so unsanitary in the way of the street vendors serving food. Hot food vendor on the street had a small wash pot to wash all the chopsticks and plates which were cleaned by dipping in the pot and dried with the washcloth. People only stayed away from street food when cholera was in the news; a few days later everything returned to the same old way.

Middle School

I followed my brothers' footsteps to Yi-an (Nghĩa-An) Middle School, where Mandarin was taught. The school was established by the people of Chaozhou, which was part of Guangdong but the dialect was entirely different from Cantonese. Chaozhou were the second populous Chinese people group in Vietnam after the Cantonese. They concentrated in the Mekong Delta, and were exposed to Vietnamese more than those of us in Cholon; between classes, those classmates talked to each other in Vietnamese, and that was an astonishing discovery for me. In biology class, when the Vietnamese teacher announced the topic "dung beetle" my classmates from the delta roared into laughter and I scratched my head bewildering at what was so funny. I had no idea what that term meant, had never seen one before; and the lesson was about the anatomy of the insect but mentioned not what it fed on and "dung" was not part of the insect's name in Vietnamese.

Chairman Ma of the School Board Trustees was wealthy and influential. In the 1963 coup d'état, President Diệm and his brother Nhu fled to seek refuge in Ma's residence, finally the brothers were snatched away and shot.

In Yi-an, I took Vietnamese elementary school exams twice and got two diplomas. The reason was that when I took the first exam, my birth certificate bore Mom's maiden name when we attempted to go to Taiwan during the naturalization crisis.

The vivid impression I got when taking the exam was the flag-raising ceremony. In front of the flag pole, boys wearing white shirts and trousers, and girls in white Vietnamese áo dài (long dresses) sang the national anthem. The boys and girls under the direction of a teacher, sang their anthem very forcefully with colorful inflections which was so different to the solemn yet rather dull anthem of the Republic of China, which lyrics were taken from the oath of Kuomintang written in clusters of four words; one needed college-level Chinese to understand the meaning of all those words.

The exam consisted of four subjects: dictation, math, science, singing or poem recitation. I chose singing for both exams. Maybe I was the only one that had two Vietnamese grade school diplomas. A Vietnamese pupil did not pass this national exam could not attend the public middle schools.

Dad's Business

Dad told us that he was a partner on name only in a food wholesale business partnership, namely he contributed nothing financially to the incorporation of the company. He was granted the partnership due to his remarkable salesmanship and integrity. He got paid a nominal monthly salary, even lower than that of a typist clerk in the company, but he was entrusted to be the key holder of the safe, from which he took as much as needed by just leaving a hand-written note.

The majority ownership was of one who started his career from the bottom up, by transporting sugar squares on bike from the family-owned sugar refinery in the countryside to Cholon. The food business grew from dry food to importing fruit, liquor, and candies; and exporting rice and cattle to Hong Kong. The company became the sole agent for Borden's powdered milk KLIM, and Japanese Ajinomoto's monosodium glutamate.

Dad's business partner was minimally educated but very smart, big and tall in stature with an imposing demeanor which I had not encountered in my life including all the V.I.P.s in the military. Yet he was very gentle and warm in meeting and encouraging us kids to study hard to achieve in life.

At the year's end Dad was busy to fulfill the orders from customers on apples, Sunkist oranges, grapes, dates, chocolates and liquors.

At home we used to have a case of red delicious apples in addition to Danish cookies, Peek Freans biscuits, Netherland butter, May Ellen jellies, Cadbury and Golden Cup chocolates, French cognac, Italian wines, and last but not least Japanese instant noodles which were unique by then.

A New House

At the final year of middle school, we moved from the alley to a three-storied house. The house was four meters by twenty meters with four-meter ceilings, plus a terrace on the fourth level. This house was huge in comparison with the old one. The house located near the thoroughfare Trần Hưng Đạo Avenue which spanned Saigon and Cholon. Two movie theaters named Oscar and Palace were five and ten minutes walking distance away. The house was two blocks from a major market so it was very convenient for groceries. From early dawn, the motorized tricycles carrying goods from truck stops to the market were already busy travelling on our street.

At the first floor of the house, we had a ping-pong table. We no longer needed to go to ping-pong clubs or played on the miniature table we improvised. We could play with friends for long hours. We played well but not good enough to win trophies.

English High School

After junior high, again following brother Ju-Jiang, I went to an English school operated by the Catholics called Free Pacific Language Institute.

For boys we wore long-sleeved white shirts and khaki trousers. On our shirts, there was an ingenious school emblem above the left pocket: embroidered in blue was a cross outlined by the four letters FPLI; F on top, P on the left, L on the right and I on the bottom to form an outline of the cross. Underneath the cross was the student number; Ju-Jiang carried E0647, E1447 was mine.

The principal was a Belgian priest with Chinese nationality named Lei Zhen-Yuan, literally thunderclap rumbles far.

He had been in China for decades before 1950, and came to Vietnam after the Communist takeover. He spoke perfect Mandarin and was a member of the Kuomintang.

The teachers were family members of the American G.I.s or graduates from universities in China, Taiwan, Hong Kong, and Germany.

By attending this school my English had been tremendously strengthened. My accent became American rather than British as previously exposed to. I used to prepare my lessons in advance, hence was actively engaging in class. On the other hand, I was motivated by a brief biography to read English out loud for half an hour daily, therefore, had been asked by a teacher to read in front of the class occasionally.

On Monday mornings, students were assembled in the big hall and lectured by Father Lei. Before school dismissal on Wednesday, each student received a loaf of baguette, which was baked with flour from U.S.A.I.D. This was ironic indeed, for the student body was from middle- or upper-class families, some were chauffeured to school in shiny Mercedes Benz.

In my class, there were two sisters who never attend Saturday classes, for they were Seventh Day Adventists. The younger sister was chubby and the older one skinny. Their uniforms were of pricey materials, and their bird nest hairstyle was unique in the school.

A Chinese teacher was from Peking University where he majored in Chinese literature, he had a classmate who could recite in entirety everything read just once, but could not compose a good paper.

Some of the American teachers I could recall were: Mrs. Adams, Mrs. Arbuckle, Mrs. Crawford, Kent and Elizabeth Foster, and Mrs. Seely. In one semester, a lower grade class had a substitute teacher that was so beautiful; boys and girls alike in the class could not concentrate on their books but kept looking at her. When the class was over, her husband in Army fatigues came to pick her up.

School Years and College

All our teachers came to teach in their huge American sedans I could not imagine how they managed to drive through the narrow and crowded streets near our school.

Bible Verses

We had an African American teacher, Mrs. Abrams, probably, who wrote in my souvenir notebook "Pride goeth before destruction and a haughty spirit before a fall. Proverb 16:18." Looking back, I thank God for moving her to give me a Bible verse hinting to what was in me.

With the American involvement in the Vietnam War, FM radio and television came to Saigon through the U.S. Armed Forces Radio and Television Services. Suddenly, we had been dragged into the modern American culture in sounds and images; it was first from its radio broadcast that I learned about the assassination of President John F. Kennedy. Everywhere in the city, the fluorescent screens attracted throngs of viewers watching TV from sunset to midnightTopics from Bonanza, Combat, Gun Smoke, Mission: Impossible, etc. became part of the daily conversation in town. I remembered vividly the finale before the TV station shutdown: it was a scene of water streaking through a rocky creek with the words "Be still and know that I am God ... Psalm 46:10." Without any prompting, I had been shown Bible verses here and there.

At the time I entered the Institute, my brother Ju-Jiang went to Taiwan for college. I joined in to correspond with his pen pal David Smith, who was then working for the Postal Service. Routinely, David sent us Time, Newsweek, U.S. News and World Report, Reader's Digest, road maps, and travel brochures of various states. I learned so many things from these materials.

The music teacher Diệp Đình Cơ at the Institute also taught at Yian. He graduated from the National Conservatory and liked to bring his violin to the class. Customarily, he used a tuning fork to tune his instrument or to set the tone by bringing the fork to his ear after hitting it on the furniture nearby. The naughty boys liked to imitate the teacher in hitting the index finger and middle finger on the desk, and then brought them close to the ear and said "La ..." In the first music class, Mr. Diệp called me to the front sing duet with him, a hymn from the Deep South I learned from him in Yian "Somebody's Knocking at Your Door". The duet was cut short when my part went out of tune against his.

A Close Friend
A classmate shared the desk with me was Sandy Chau and we became good friends; later on he went to study in Berkeley. We lost touch for a long time until Sandy returned to Saigon with Ruth his newlywed to develop an industrial park on Saigon's riverfront. Sandy sought my help but it was impossible when I was in the military and faraway. One day I went home on furlough, when walking into the door abruptly Dad told me that I had lost a friend! I was astonished to learn that as Sandy was trusting in our sincere friendship therefore entrusted a business opportunity to my brother's brother-in-law who turned it into a treacherous deal. Henceforth my relationship with Sandy became history. Sandy had been a successful businessman and entrepreneur in the San Francisco area.

Fleeting Blues
After dinner and homework, occasionally I went to the balcony or the terrace looking up to the starry sky. The dark night sky impressed in me the vastness and depth of the universe. I went downtown Saigon to the British Council borrowed a couple books on radio astronomy. The dimension of the universe, the astronomical size and number of galaxies, and the assured demise of our Milky Way led to moments of melancholy on the minuteness of man. Were we merely to be born, growing up, getting old, and fading into oblivion?

Changing Tastes

In the formative times, my aim in life shifted from teaching geography (through an inspiring book propounding that by teaching others about geography could bring mutual appreciation and peace to the world), to piloting a fighter plane, astronomy, agriculture and medicine.

Chinese High School

After a year and a half in the Free Pacific Language Institute, I switched to a Chinese high school to prepare to go to Taiwan.

I graduated in 1964 from the Chinese school and was granted admission to the National Taiwan University to study agricultural engineering. Now the escalation of the war resulted in stricter criterion for study abroad, the Chinese high school diploma was not qualified any more but that of the Vietnamese or the French.

Vietnamese diplomas were granted only through national exams. Its high school diploma consisted of Part I and II. Therefore, I had to spend two additional years for two Vietnamese high school exams. Legendarily, graduation ratio was thirty percent for Part I, and within these only another thirty percent passed the Part II. A student did not have Part I diploma could not enter the twelfth grade, even in private schools.

Vietnamese High Schools

In order to prepare for the Part I exam, I went to a private school two blocks away from home for evening classes. The school was small with only five classrooms. The two neon lights hung on the ceiling of the class for forty students worsened my nearsightedness.

The school was owned and operated by Mr. Lý văn Hùng, a well-known teacher through the Vietnamese teaching broadcasts for Cantonese on the Voice of Vietnam. He was very good in both languages and had coauthored a Chinese-Vietnamese dictionary which was unique in its category. In junior high, my Chinese teacher demonstrated the musical reading of Chinese poems; here Principal Lý exhibited his skill in reciting the Vietnamese and Cantonese poetry. Mr. Lý was a heavy-smoker of the British brand "State Express 555"; he smoked in front of the class without apology. Mr. Lý smoked the imported cigarette for all its worth: he inhaled deeply and held the smoke inside, when the smoke finally came out of his nostrils, it was barely visible.

After finishing my Part I education, I went to Saigon to attend Hưng Đạo School which was also Catholic-run.

Vietnamese Curriculum

The Vietnamese school system consisted of five years of elementary, four years of junior high and three years of senior high. The Vietnamese system offered three foci of study in the eleventh and twelfth grades: Experimental Sciences, Mathematics, and Liberal Arts. Since I had taken all the science and math courses in Chinese high school, I picked the third one, so that could learn more Vietnamese.

Profiles of Teachers

The core curriculum of Liberal Arts in Twelve Grade consisted of four components: psychology, logics, metaphysics and ethics. Teacher of the first three segments was Father Trần văn Hiến Minh who held a doctorate from La Sorbonne. He was humorous but not very good in transmitting knowledge. One thing I learned from this course was that psychology was scientific in the realm of sensory experimentations, but subjective in the notions of human experiences.

The teacher of ethics was Father Trần Đức Huynh who gave talks ranging from his trips to the U.S. to politics but nothing on the subject that he was supposed to teach. His accent was so thick that I could not understand even his travelogue. As it turned out, in the national exams no questions besides psychology were given. I bumped into Father Huynh in a Catholic church in Silver Spring, Maryland in 1980. When the Mass was over, I went to greet the teacher that I had not seen for more than a decade. I was dumbfounded when he responded to my greetings with "Have you bought a house yet?"

I took some classes in French then dropped out although it was part of the paid package, for it required efforts to memorize the grammatical inflections. I remembered teacher Roc Cường said that after teaching French for thirty years, he was no more certain of the gender of words by the incessant queries from his students.

The teacher of physiology was Dr. Quan Quảng Hoa the personal physician to an influential General.

In my English class, there were several students with very good English including two brothers who had passed the Lower Diploma from Cambridge. Not that far into the first class, the older brother queried arrogantly the teacher on the structure of the "absolute sentence" but the teacher shot back and told him to behave. The teacher, Dr. Uông Ngọc Thạch was not just another M.D. who liked to teach in his spare time, but a special assistant to President Thiệu. The school really had so many uncommon teachers.

Minor Accident

One day I was riding my moped to school, a Lambro three-wheel passenger vehicle swerved into my path to pick up a customer on the sidewalk. It happened so abrupt that I had to steer my moped to avoid the collision, my front wheel hit the curb and I was airborne and landing on all four on the sidewalk. The Lambro sped up and skipped the customer. I got some minor scrapes on my palms and broke a large piece of skin below my left kneecap, the scar remained visible till now.

During the school year, there was an opportunity to go to America attending college for free. The Ministry of Education held a national exam on English, and three finalists would get a four-year scholarship. I was approved by the school to take the exam. The title of the written exam was: "Hope is the dream of a man awake" (a French proverb). Somehow, only a female student won the second place.

Then I had another hemorrhoid surgery which was done by Daddy's friend Dr. Đặng Ngọc Tùng, in the top hospital of Vietnam—Chợ Rẫy Hospital. Chợ Rẫy means vegetable market, but Chinese called it "Big Water Towers Hospital" which situated next to several humongous water towers.

Post-Surgery Hemorrhage

During the week of convalescence at home, one day I strained too hard in a bowel movement and bleeding started after midnight. I was awakened by intestinal spasms and found myself in a pool of blood. I was driven to Chợ Rẫy Hospital by Dr. Tùng in his Fiat; it was curfew time only certain people could travel in that period, and physicians were among them.

As I was waiting in the triage area, a young man was put on the adjacent bed with a grenade wound. His white shirt was sticking to his abdomen soaked with blood, a male nurse or medical intern injected something into his midsection by a syringe with a very long needle while he was moaning continuously.

At that moment, I was pushed away to a surgery ward. It was cold in the room and quite soon I went into shock: my entire body trembled and I saw things doubling up. I tried hard to refocus by shaking my head, it worked but immediately double vision returned. Quickly, I was pushed to the ICU and a couple nurses set on me a blanketed wire cage strung with many high-wattage lightbulbs, and a shot was injected into my calf. After a while, I recovered from the

School Years and College

shivering. I stayed in the hospital for two days and returned a month later to have remedial surgery.

I missed school for two months, I brought the discharge paper to the school's business office to resume my class otherwise I had to pay up the full tuition of the months of absence. Unlike the public schools where fees were minimal, private high schools required monthly tuition payments.

Erroneously I believed that even if I had my diploma Part II, I needed a full-attendance record for the application to study abroad. Therefore, the rational thing I should do was to stay in school for another year. Just for fun I took the national exam without any preparation. Of course I flunked, but missed the passing mark just by two points.

A year later I passed the Part II. Exam results were categorized by grade points, D was passable and that was what most people got, only a handful got A's, and mine was C which was pretty good, I comforted myself.

The legal age in Vietnam was based on the year of birth not by date. I was born at the end of the year and was counted as nineteen when I got my high school diploma. The age limit for overseas study had been lowered to eighteen, which was also the draft age for military service. The only choice I had was to stay and attend domestic colleges.

Pharmacy School

I wanted to go to medical school, but our family friend Dr. Tùng advised me that more than half the courses in medical school would be taught in French, and he did not think I could handle it. He proposed that I would go after pharmacy.

The top name for higher learning was the University of Saigon, which consisted of the Colleges of Medicine, Dentistry, Pharmacy, Sciences, Law, and Liberal Arts. Besides, there were the Phú Thọ Engineering School, Teachers College and School of Agriculture, Forestry and Husbandry. Besides the Sciences, Law, and Liberal Arts, all colleges in the University of Saigon required entrance examination: Medical School accepted 200 students per year, Pharmacy 400, and Dentistry fifty, each from more than 10,000 applicants.

Pharmacist was a profession of leisure, after obtaining the degree one just opened a pharmacy and hired people to run it. All medicines including antibiotics were available over the counter, only controlled substances were dispensed through prescription.

The first year Pharmacy students took only two classes in the school: Inorganic and Organic Chemistry. The professor of the inorganic chemistry class was a PhD from Montpellier University in France. The professor of organic chemistry was a lady who earned the first doctorate of science from the University of Saigon. The remainder of the study was pharmacy internship in a pharmacy, public or private pharmacy. I followed the advice of Dr. Tùng to take my internship at Chợ Rẫy Hospital, the most prestigious hospital of the Republic.

The Tet Offensive

Then it was the lunar New Year of 1968 and the earth-shaking Tết Offensive. Taking advantage of the New Year ceasefire the Vietcong forces carried out surprise attacks all over the South. Lunar New Year time was the sacred holiday period of the Vietnamese, this blatant violation caught the South off guard; even the U.S. Marines guarding the American Embassy suffered losses from the attack.

A few months later, in May a second-wave attack of Vietcong came to the heart of Cholon. Helicopters fired machine guns and rockets above rooftops, F-4 Phantom fighter-bombers strafed 20mm cannons on targets around the city, and B-52 Stratofortress bombings rumbled in the distance.

All male college students were called up to form the Division of College Students to Defend the Capital. We reported to respective campuses to get khaki uniforms and armed with carbines or Thompson submachine guns along with a single cartridge of bullets. We were trained by the cadets from the Thủ Đức Infantry School in basic military parade and formation. Students of the Military Medicine School came to teach battlefield first aid. We were trucked to security posts at various buildings around Cholon.

General Mobilization

The expanding warfare in the entire South demanded more soldiers, therefore a general mobilization was decreed, and deferment criteria tightened. Before the Tết Offensive, male college students could stay in school till twenty five, now freshmen could not be older than twenty. So I had to report for military service.

Some suggested that I should join the Navy as a sailor to shun combat duty; or enter the National Police, but nobody really liked to be in the Police even as officer, for it carried a stigma of corruption and draft evasion; or flee to Hong Kong and stay out of the war for good, which would cost my Father a fortune and the future was unpredictable.

My eldest brother Ju-Hua was a corporal in the Army Corps of Engineers stationed close to Saigon, by his personal experience in the military that there was a huge difference between an enlisted man and an officer, therefore I decided to be an officer.

Chapter 3.

Military Life

Report to Duty

On March 7, 1969, in the early afternoon, the three of us who failed the deferment requirement, Trần Ken my Pharmacy classmate, Lư Tô from the College of Science, and I took a taxicab to the Capital Military Command, from which we and dozens of draftees were trucked to the Enlistment Center Number Three in Hóc Môn.

First Twenty-Four Hours

The Center was surrounded by watchtowers and barbed wires; it looked more like a detention compound than for prospective freedom fighters, because many draftees got there involuntarily, therefore escapes happened frequently.

In the camp all the people stayed together without any distinction between future officers and soldiers,

From the tin roof shacks, crude wooden bunk beds, prison-guard type personnel, to the vitamin B1 supplemented yellow-colored rice and fried dried fish that was my first-day impression of my six years fourteen days military career. When I was recalling this forty some years later, I realized how luxurious was that kind of meal in contrast to those in the POW, "reeducation", and refugee camps.

A crowd of several hundred inductees were gathered to listen to a loud 2nd Lt. who emphasized discipline under his command. He claimed that no matter who you were if you were disobedient he could make your life very harsh. Next day, an incident happened near our perimeter; that Lt. was yelling as loud as he could, to reprimand a Corporal for not saluting him. It lasted for a few minutes and left me with a very bad taste. If that was not a staged act to impress us, it would be unthinkable in the military. If the latter proved to be the case, what a portending of discipline breakdown in the final days of ARVN!

After rejecting the mess hall provision, we three bought our own dinners from a food stall. Later on the entire group was led to a big open field to watch a live show. Camp shows in the ARVN were under the auspices of the Directorate of Psychological Warfare. The only thing I remembered from the show was the name of a songstress Phương Hồng Quế, for it resembled that of the famous Phương Hồng Hạnh. Quế became a famous Vietnamese entertainer in the States after 1975.

During the night, we lined up for physical checkup. Everybody stripped down to his shorts and walked past a military physician for an inspection of hernia. After the five-second screening we went to a clothing booth to find out our shoe sizes by sticking the right foot into a row of boots which had the posterior sections removed. Then, each one of us was issued fatigues, underwear, socks, belt, cap, knapsack, and a pair of black canvas boots. I put my civilian clothing into my hand bag and used it as pillow. Spending a night on the wooden bunk bed, I did not get bitten by bed bug as I had feared. I tossed and turned the whole night, not only because of rumor of thieves but also the uncertainties of the future.

First Furlough

The next morning, we were gathered after washing. Those who were going to the Officer Candidate School (OCS) got a seven days' leave, all the rest went to the Quang Trung Training Center—the largest ARVN boot camp.

In our one-size-fits-all uniforms, I hopped on a Lambro at the entrance of the camp. Going home was such a relief after just one day in the military.

My younger brother Ju-Fang drove me back on a scooter to the Enlistment Center after the first ever furlough. Before noon we were trucked to the Quang Trung Center. It was March 16, 1969; on the same day six years later, I began my exit from the military, involuntarily.

Nguyễn Huệ Battalion

The basic training lasted for nine weeks. I had no idea how many trainee battalions were there at the Center, but one battalion was reserved for the pre-OCS cadets; that battalion was named after Nguyễn Huệ, i.e. Emperor Quang Trung of the Nguyễn Dynasty, a national hero.

The Nguyễn Huệ Battalion was famous for its discipline, because we were destined to lead. My first impression of the Battalion perimeter was tidiness, with an impressive sight of the trenches looked like those made out of concrete; pretty soon we were shown how to use our mess kits to create that look. Coming along was a sense of forlornness by the Spartan and minimalistic settings, I had stepped on a vastly different path of life.

Trần Ken, Lư Tô and I did not get back as a group henceforth we wound up in different companies and missing out each other from then on. I met Lư Tô eight years later at the Bù Gia Mập "reeducation" camp in Phước-Long.

Military Life

Starting a Friendship

In the afternoon, the first roll call and line-up. With a height of 1.67 meters or 5'7", I ended up at the tall end of the company of 200. During the process, a guy asked me to switch my spot with his friend; my response was negative, and he was somewhat annoyed. I did not recognize him as a Chinese, likewise he could not detect my accent or the look of a Sino-Vietnamese. Not too much later that guy Vương Chiêu became my fast buddy and we maintained a lifelong friendship ever since. Chiêu studied in the College of Science; he volunteered to join the Navy as Ken did. After the basic training, they would report to the Navy.

Basic Training

The first lesson in formation and parade was a little bit different from what I had learned in the Boy Scouts. The military 360 degree about-face had two steps instead of three; I thought the three-step way of the Boy Scouts made the turn easier and neater.

I felt depressed sometimes. If I were born only a month later I would still be in school! I had no idea where I would wind up. Would I be assigned to combat duty? Would I station far away from Saigon?

Around us, we saw the steep contrast between the lethargic conscripts and the volunteering paratroopers. The professional soldiers jogged to and fro between the barracks and the field classes; they shouted frequently "Airborne destroys enemies, KILL!"

We were vaccinated for cholera and took sulfadiazine against meningitis from a dispensing station. The pills were taken with water from a rusty fifty-five gallon drum.

Mannerism of Officers

Our company commander Lt. Hải had a student-like demeanor and gentle way of speaking. He reminded us to keep a package containing a needle, some threads and a couple of buttons in the shirt pocket, for we as officers have to keep our uniforms in good shape, in the presence of superiors as well as subordinates; the package would come in handy when a button was missing or coming loose.

Many folks brought their fatigues to the base tailor shops for alteration, but I had no need to do that, the standard size fit me nicely.

Our outfits were primarily from the States; only the fatigues, underwear, and canvas boots were produced domestically. The one inconvenience we had were the lacking of liner bands for our helmets: when jogging in full gear, we wore our caps under the helmets but still had to spare a hand to keep the helmet in place. I did not get the helmet liner band until arriving at my post.

Handling the Rifle

We learned to handle our basic weapon, the service rifle Garand M-1. In order to load or unload a clip of bullets, at first, I had to stand the rifle on the ground, and used all my might to press down its operating rod. After handling the rifle for a couple weeks continuously, moving the rod downwards became nothing by the edge of my palm. The weighty rifle gradually more felt like an extension of my arms, bayonet practice and rifle twirling were fun and easy.

One day, it was twelve noon in the firing range, we were ordered to lie down and aim; the sands under my belly felt like boiling water. I shuddered when I read about our soldiers wearing biological warfare gears fought in the 130 degree desert of Iraq.

On a few Sundays that we were not permitted to go home, my brothers would come to see me with home-cooked food and snacks. We shared our food with those who did not have visitors.

Military Life

Nine weeks went by fast, we graduated without any ceremony. A few people returned to their government agencies; the rest of us got a one-week leave.

Officer Candidate School

A week later, from Quang Trung boot camp we were transported twenty miles in military trucks to the OCS known as the Infantry School of Thủ Đức.

After passing by the School Headquarters and the parade ground, the trucks stopped at our designated battalion's compound. We were welcomed on the scene by some senior cadets. They looked very sharp wearing purplish blue berets with khaki uniforms; pinned on their right pockets were engraved nametags, on their shoulders black velvet epaulets with bronze alphas, dangling from their left shoulder straps the red-yellow unit medallion tassels and on their feet spit-shined boots. Carrying the duffle bags on our shoulders, we were harassed around by the loud orders erupted from those cadets. Some were ordered to stand in attention, while others were doing pushups, and after ten minutes of controlled chaos, five groups were formed and each one marched to a company compound.

Cadet Company

My cadet company for the next six months was Forty Third Company of the Third Class of 1969 or Class of 3/69. Our Company Commander was 1st Lt. Hiển whom later was promoted to Capt. and discharged to serve in the Ministry of Agriculture. The other three officers were: 1st Lt. Nguyễn văn Ba, a Đà Lạt Military Academy graduate, 2nd Lt. Nguyễn văn Sang, a graduate of Fort Benning OCS in Georgia, and CWO i.e. Commissioned Warrant Officer Thân Trọng Tuệ, my platoon leader graduated recently from Fort Benning.

Nine Months

Under the strenuous responsibility to produce a constant supply of infantry officers to the ARVN, our training course including the basic training that we had just finished spanning nine months. The first thing in the OCS was to go through a period of minor-scale hazing called "Eight Weeks of Humiliation Education", during which we jogged everywhere in the School, were to obey all the orders from senior cadets, and no furlough on weekend.

Open Shaming

Nearly every morning, we jogged in formation for a few miles with intermittent stretching exercise and pushups. One morning after returning to the Company ground, I was singled out by CWO Tuệ for additional pushups: because the lower front of my undershirt was smeared with dirt. All the physical punishment, even intentionally unfair was for building endurance and obedience to orders, but I hated to be seen as a jerk and humiliated in front of the Company. I knew that after having taken a couple years of track drill in the Cộng Hòa Stadium, my condition should be better than the average guys: I could do thirty chin-ups and pulled the chest expander of six rubber bands. That morning I was doing my pushups earnestly that my sweaty undershirt got away from the cheap shorts and licked up dirt. Besides, no one else had been picked before or afterwards.

A couple years later, Tuệ along with a dozen or so cadets were killed by a claymore mine on the way to a field class. What a tragedy!

Punishment Night

On another occasion, I went to the Cộng Hòa General Hospital to check out my bleeding hemorrhoids. When I came back in the afternoon, I was ordered to report for an evening of field exercise in full gear, because the dorm's floor was dirty that day, but supposedly my duty on that day should be relieved due to sick leave. My "lone ranger" marching and push-ups ended by midnight, either the administering officer was tired or he knew that I was having hemorrhoid problem.

Baguette and Banana

During the first eight weeks, in the morning, the cadets-on-duty brought back, in a poncho, our breakfast of French baguettes and (ripened and bruised) bananas. Everyone ate lunch and dinner in the mess hall, under the supervision of four senior cadets who rotated on a weekly basis.

The Alpha

Finishing the eight humiliation education weeks, we earned an Alpha on the chest of the fatigues between the second and third buttons, and salaried as a sergeant.

After qualified as cadets, we had more leeway for meals. The majority of us no more ate at the mess hall, instead we went to the "family restaurants" operated by the soldiers' and NCOs' families near the mess hall. That was a good way to supplement their incomes.

We got furloughs on some of the weekends when there were no security alerts; for those occasions we put on the khaki uniforms and visor caps. We were dropped off and picked up in Saigon's Central Market by GMC trucks.

We spent our nights only once in a while in our barracks, usually we slept in the bunkers or in the open air adjacent to the guarding posts within the school perimeter. Not only it was necessary for us to get used to the life in the battlefield but also our barracks were targets of enemy mortars. After our night watch duties, we slept in hammocks inside the machinegun nests or underground silos. Once we stayed in front of a 105mm howitzer battery; the gun blasts and wind gusts from the cannon muzzles flattened all our tents, but we were so tired we could go back to sleep quickly after the stirs.

Night of Steel

On one occasion we were to have a weapon inspection in the morning. After our rifles had been cleaned inside and out, the rain came. My group of four set up the tent, rolled up our rifles in a poncho and slept on them. I twisted and turned the whole night.

Opportunity Lost

One day, I overslept in an underground machinegun bunker and the platoon left without me. On that morning I had been scheduled to take an English qualification test. When I rushed to the classroom, the test had already begun. I sat at the rear of the room and the magnetic tape deck in the front was hard to hear, so I could not answer many of the questions. Those who passed the test would be assigned to the Military Foreign Language School near Saigon.

In another occasion, I was informed that I was one of several candidates as aide-de-camp to Lt. Gen. Vĩnh Lộc, Commandant of the Training Directorate. Eventually no one was picked probably our zodiac signs were incompatible with the General's.

Field Classes

The majority of our training classes were outside of the Infantry School perimeter. We went out under a tall guard tower equipped with M-2 heavy machine guns, and then we formed a single file walked through the villages and rice paddies. Although we were protected by soldiers from the OCS' organic unit, we had to keep distance from each other, so that a single bullet could not penetrate a dozen of us. With a cadet company of 200, it took almost thirty minutes for us to assemble for lesson.

Women and children selling snacks, cold drinks and sweet soups were always present around the field classrooms. When we were in doubt of pinpointing the right signpost among a row of them in our lensatic compass exercises, those kids had all the answers.

Tuxedo

A few weeks before graduation, tailors from the Quartermasters came to measure and sew us tuxedos for the ceremony. That was the only tailored uniform I ever had.

There was a movie theater in the OCS named Purple Eve, I did not recall if I had been there. Leisure time was precious; we could fool around only in the last few days before graduation.

Scary Folklore

In the ARVN there were a great deal of folklore, such as the statue of the sad soldier at the entrance of Biên Hòa Military Cemetery, it knocked at doors asking for water. In the same vein, on the OCS parade ground, there was the Tower of the Loyal and Righteous. As a tradition, the graduating class would post honor guards at the memorial on the eve of graduation; the honor guards would encounter spirits of the departed officers coming back to visit. I had not been picked for that honor.

Final Evening and Day

The last evening in the OCS, we seven good buddies in the company went to the Cadet's Club to drink. It was the first time I got drunk after downing seven bottles of "33"-brand beers.

Lackluster Graduation

For some reason Company Forty Three did not take part in the graduation ceremony and missed out our most memorable event. That morning, a few NCOs walking around with Polaroid cameras to take pictures, I paid 500 piasters (one dollar) got mine taken in beige-colored tuxedo with visor cap and black velvet waistband.

Before noon, we got paid and handed our two-week furlough and notices of service branches to report to. I felt relieved to be assigned to the Medical Service Corps like others who flunked medicine or pharmacy. But there were exceptions: Phạm văn Hiền my classmate went to the Ordnance, a medical student to the Artillery. Probably, the assignments had something do to with the psychological/talent test that we took.

The Omega

It was the first and last time that we could roam around in the School compounds. After taking off our tuxedos and changed into fatigues, we went to the shops to purchase our own brass omegas for CWO. We tore away the cloth alphas on our chests and pinned two shining omegas on our collars. It was a time of mixed emotions, happy because the training was over, sad because we would miss the many friends we made after nine months and probably would never see each other again. After an hour of saying goodbyes, we boarded the GMC trucks with our duffle bags and going back to Saigon. Farewell! Infantry School of Thủ Đức.

Military Medicine School

Two weeks later I reported to the Military Medicine School which was about four miles from home.

Our class had forty guys. The assignment of our military specialties depended largely on the demand of the time, we were fortunate to be Administrative Officers who worked behind the desks. Some classes were trained to be Auxiliary Medical Officers or Nursing Officers, the former would take care of field medicine at the battalion level.

We did take some classes on general medicine but our emphasis was on administrative duties.

Military Life

The Commandant of the School was Naval Surgeon Capt. Phạm Vận, the only person wearing navy blue uniform in the sea of olive green fatigues. We saw him mostly in the Monday morning flag raising ceremony.

The strictest discipline in this School was the short haircut, shorter than the boot camp and OCS. All officers in training wore berets instead of the Army cap. On our purplish-blue berets from the OCS, we replaced the beret flash of "Sword and Sacred Flame" with the "Staff of Asclepius."

Some staff members were in their fifties; the silver plum flowers for the ranks of Lt. Col. and Maj. they wore were not silvery bright but smoky dark. In the School, besides the offices and classrooms were dormitories for the cadets of Military Medicine; they attended the civilian medical, pharmacy, or dental school in military uniform. The cadets got paid a salary of either 1st or 2nd Lt. These cadets would someday be commanders of military medicine units.

During that period, there was another Administrative Officer's class of about thirty old folks; they were NCOs who had been in the Medical Service for so long and got promoted to officers. While we young officers tried not to brag about our junior rank but these old folks like to show off their ranks by getting the largest insignia available, some even pinned the omegas from the epaulets of Naval officers on their collars. Later on I served under one of these folks for a year.

Near Head-On Collision

On an afternoon, our class ended at three as usual and dismissed. I was riding my scooter on Nguyễn Tri Phương Street which was famous for the numerous eateries and food stands on the sidewalks.

A rainstorm was imminent and raindrops began to fall, so I sped up trying to get home before the downpour. I was going at about forty mph. From the curb, a food vendor took a pail of water splashed it across the road in their customary dishwater disposal. It was too late for me to shun the water; my scooter hydroplaned and glided at an angle to the other side of the road. At that moment, my scooter headed toward a blue Air Force Dodge ambulance that was approaching. The converging of so many things unexpectedly and I could not come up with any response to the crisis; all I did was shut tightly my eyes and let what should happen to happen.

Thump! I felt no impact but found myself sitting on the road next to my scooter which was lying on its side, and my eyeglasses flew several feet away. The ambulance driver and his companion rushed to my side and helped me to stand up. I picked up my glasses, looked around and found nothing wrong, I thanked them and the soldiers departed happily.

I pulled the scooter to the roadside and wondering if I should go to punch the guy who splashed the water to teach him a lesson; in no time I decided to let it go because I did not get hurt at all. A classmate on his Honda motorcycle went by and stopped to check on me. I tried to kick start the scooter and it did not work, so I asked my buddy to tow me to a repair shop by grasping on his right shoulder with my left hand.

The repair shop found out that the scooter was unable to start because the neck of the sparkplug was snapped. It was incredible that I got no injury, my glasses were intact, and the scooter did not have visible scraping or dent, while all the force of impact ended up on a sparkplug. I dared not imagine what would happen if I had taken action at that instant in any other way.

Predicting the Future

My fast buddy since boot camp Vương Chiêu was still a Naval Cadet in the Navy Language School awaiting training in the U.S. We always went out together on the weekends. On one of those days, we went to a famous female fortune-teller to see what were lying ahead of us. Looking back years later the predictions were somewhat accurate on a few things.

After reading our palms, she predicted that in the not too distant future Chiêu would go to a foreign country but not me; and my rank could not go beyong 1st Lt. I thought that was not too bad at all, I might be discharged before becoming a Captain.

Selection of Unit

Seven months of the Military Medicine School concluded with unit selection. In the classroom, on the blackboard was an outline map of South Vietnam showing unit openings. The order of selection was determined by score ranking which were not known until the name was read.

It was a nerve-wracking moment, the sooner one got called there would the better choices. The first guy picked the apparent top choice—his former unit—the Saigon Naval Hospital. I was placed in the middle of the class and the two units among the remaining I preferred were: Duy Tân General Hospital in Đà Nẵng of I Corps, or Seventy Second Medical Group in Pleiku of II Corps. A General Hospital was located in big city but stressful duty-wise and hard to get furloughs; so I chose the Medical Group, which was comparatively relaxed, and the Commander of II Corps Lt. Gen. Lữ Lan was a good friend of Dr. Tùng.

Pleiku on the Highlands

Two weeks after graduation, my classmate Phan Ngọc Lang and I boarded an Air Vietnam DC-6 to fly to Pleiku.

The flight lasted an hour, and the plane landed around two o'clock in the afternoon. Following the other passengers, I walked to the exit door, a draft of cold air rushed in. I knew Pleiku was on the Central Highlands, but did not expect it was cold in August. I looked through the door, there was a rusty mountain chain standing against a backdrop of blue sky. I felt weirdly lost and homesick, wanted to turn back and fly home.

The plane parked next to the civilian air terminal which was a very small one-story concrete building, and there were a few people, several cars and Jeeps.

We boarded the Air Vietnam bus went on a two-lane highway flanked by vast grassland atop the reddish volcanic dirt, scattered here and there were small corrugated tin houses. The bus went by a circle which was surrounded by houses, shops and a movie theater called Diệp Kính, obviously a Chinese name. The bus turned left and, stopped at the Air Vietnam office. We picked up our suitcases and I called Phạm văn Hiền, my Pharmacy and OCS classmate, at the Pleiku Ammunition Depot using a hand-cranked field telephone in the office.

Hiền and his driver picked us up in a Jeep and backtracking the way we came in. After all, our units were not that far from the airfield.

They dropped Lang off at the Pleiku Military Hospital which was neighboring my unit. Between the two units were some barbed wire fences and a strip of land housing a Mortuary Platoon, but it took a couple miles of driving between the two entrances.

Then I got off at the Medical Group.

Seventy Second Medical Group

All the roads in the compound were laid over with crushed stones. The headquarters consisted of two cross-shaped Quonset hutches, underneath the unit's sign and in front of the hutches were rows of marigold. My first impression of the place was somehow unpleasant, for in my superstitious mind these flowers were used in funerals and on altars of the deceased.

The front entrance was boarded up behind the unit sign; I turned to the left and walked to a side entrance. I opened the screen door and saw a handsome 2nd Lt. sat behind a desk, I saluted him and we shook hands. Before I opened my mouth, the ever-smiling Lt. Dương Thành Điệu told me that they were expecting me for quite some times already. Điệu led me inside and introduced me to Maj. Quách văn Lang the Executive Officer. After a short chat, the Major called in an NCO to do my paperwork. The Commanding Officer of the Medical Group, Surgeon Lt. Col. Phạm Gia Tự was not in the office but seeing patients in his private clinic in town.

M.Sgt. Lê Mai Lộ was a short thin guy with a large single front tooth on the top. He said that I was a V.I.P. because the Chief of Staff of the II Corps General, Lt. Col. Nguyễn văn Giọng had called to find out my status.

Lt. Điệu drove me to the BOQ—Bachelor Officers' Quarters a hundred yards from the office. He showed me my room which was occupied by the departing Officer of Personnel 2nd Lt. Nguyễn Thanh Sơn. Sơn was on leave before transferring to the Naval Hospital in Saigon. Sơn graduated along with Điệu from the OCS, they both flunked the third year Pharmacy. Sơn was the brother of Navy Capt., eventual Commodore, Nguyễn Thanh Châu, and Commander of the one and only Naval Fleet.

History of the Group

Seventy Second Medical Group was established in 1969 and inherited the facilities from the 283rd Medical Detachment (Air Ambulance or Dustoff), U.S. Army Forty Fourth Medical Group. The compound consisted of: two Quonset huts; a helicopter landing pad and four revetments built with perforated steel planking; two-storied wooden barrack one on each end of the compound; a vacant clubhouse; a motor pool and a fuel depot. It was surrounded by barbed wire fences and several watchtowers.

Next to the concrete steps leading to the clubhouse were two olive green helicopter blades inserted to the ground in the shape of a vee; the one on the right, at eye level were these words inscribed in white paint:

So that others may live ...
Arvid O. Silverberg
Sylvester Davis
Wm Roy Henderson
Robert Sloppye

The Dustoff crew was killed by a rocket propelled grenade in a medevac mission in 1969.

Unit Hierarchy

Our Group was the highest medical unit of II Corps commanding all the military medicine units in Military Region Two from the Central Highlands to the coastal plain. We supervised four military hospitals with 400-plus beds in the cities of Pleiku, Qui Nhơn, Nha Trang (Nguyễn Huệ), and Phan Thiết (Đoàn Mạnh Hoạch); the Twenty Second and Twenty Third Military Medicine Battalions; and forty two Sectoral Dispensaries which were headed by NCO medics.

The Medical Group had many organic units including six 100-bed Sector Hospitals in the provinces of Phú Bổn, Phú Yên, Ninh Thuận, Tuyên Đức, Quảng Đức, and Lâm Đồng; two Convalescence Centers in Nha Trang and Cam Ranh; Field Hospital Number Two in Kontum; Medical Supply Depot 721 in Pleiku and 751 in Nha Trang; Veterinary Detachment Two in Qui Nhơn and Five in Nha Trang. Medical Company 722 and Ambulance Company Number Two were situated within the Medical Group's perimeter.

We also carried out basic medics training and coordination of fix-winged aircraft Medevac. Medical Company 722 situated within our compound took care of the Dispensary and Maternity Ward of II Corps Headquarters.

Our compound sprawled horizontally on a gentle slope facing the Air Force Base called Cù Hanh Air Base, therefore, we situated under the flight path of rockets attacking the air base. The II Corps Headquarters was to our left.

Pleiku was very small. It was a town surrounded by a multitude of military units. Seventy Second Medical Group as part of the region's nerve center was under the security umbrella of the II Corps Headquarters, such as: Second Air Force Division, Ranger Battalions, Special Forces, Second Calvary Regiment, Thirty Seventh and Sixty Ninth Artillery Battalions, and battalions of Regional Forces.

Fierce battles of the region in Dakto, Chuprong, Ia Drang Valley, Pleime, and Chupao, happened one or two years before I came.

Section one or S1 that I took on was in charge of Personnel and Security; it was part of the Headquarters Company which managed the operation of the Group, Surgeon Captain Nguyễn Đức Chánh was the Commander. The Medical Group was young, therefore its structure and involvement were still in flux; organic unit such as Medical Company 721 had been assigned to Dakto, later merged with Second Field Hospital.

Insubordination?

A couple days later, I stayed away from a big trouble. In that evening Lt. Điệu and I were waiting for dinner in the diner operated by the wife of Maj. Lang. CWOs Giáp the Officer of Supplies and Thanh the Medics Trainee Company Commander stopped by our table asked if I would go out with them in their Dodge ambulance (because we did not have enough Jeeps for all the officers according to the T.O.E.— Table of Organization and Equipment, so Giáp used an ambulance for transportation), somehow I did not feel like going out with strangers, so I declined.

That evening, they were detained by the Military Police for disorderly conduct against a superior. The reason was that Giáp and Thanh knew that Surgeon Capt. Đặng Hữu Phước, head of Medical Company 722, had taken surplus medical supplies from the U.S. Advisors. They went to confront Dr. Phước for the matter, the ensuing heated argument got Giáp and Thanh into trouble. They were sentenced to one year imprisonment by a Military Tribunal.

Soon after the incident Dr. Phước transferred to Saigon.

After serving times in the Military Prison in Nha Trang, Giáp and Thanh were re-assigned to the infantry. One day, Thanh dropped by our BOQ before heading to the frontline of Dakto.

Work Routine

Documents came to the Medical Group were receipt stamped and went to the X.O. who wrote down his observation or instruction, the papers in turn went by the Headquarters Company Commander, and C.O., then distributed to the relevant Sections within the Company. I spent a few minutes browsing through the teletype documents about personnel transfer or security alert; the upkeep of all the personnel records were taken care of by the staff NCOs and soldiers. After cleaning out my desk, I wandered around or played ping-pong.

Office of the MACV Medical Advisory Team was adjacent to Section One. Once a while I chatted with a few guys there, and pretty soon people noticed my English capability.

In less than a month after I came to Pleiku, I was summoned to the C.O.'s office; Dr. Tự told me that a staffer of Gen. Lan informed him that Dr. Tùng, our family friend, was experiencing some medical problem and wondered if I would like to visit him? The next day, I was back in Saigon on a two-week leave. Yes, Dr. Tùng did have some minor issues with his feet and was getting better.

A Tragic Death

A fortnight after returning to the unit, on the evening of September 17, two days after the Chinese Mid-Autumn Festival also the Vietnamese Children's Day, I went to the clubhouse and fastened a nylon hammock to the veranda to enjoy a highland sunset. From this vantage point there was the view of

Military Life

a setting sun in the purplish mountain range spreading behind the grasslands. The scenery was so serene, the increasing cold breeze made me nostalgic.

It was about six o'clock, suddenly I felt hot in my heart along with it a strange feeling of unease, some inexplicable worries were concentrated on my younger brother Ju-Fang.

Approximately at eight, a soldier came and knocked at my door: An urgent phone call was waiting for me in the headquarters.

It was from my cousin who worked for the American contractor RMK. He told me that I should try to go home because Fang had passed away due to a traffic accident. The time he expired in the hospital was 6:00 p.m.!

Needless to say, I was totally shaken up. I just saw him two weeks ago and told him to be sober when he came home drunk one night, now he was dead. I looked at the picture of my teen brother and wishing that I could see his handsome face one last time. I wept on and off through the night.

Early next morning, Lt. Điệu drove me to the C.O.'s private clinic and requested his signature on my emergency furlough. Then we turned around and went to the Air Vietnam office down the main street to purchase a ticket. Four weeks ago I was on an exciting trip home but this time for my brother's funeral. Arriving Saigon at four in the afternoon, after a short rest at home my youngest brother Ju-Xiang drove me to the funeral home.

Brother Ju-Fang was not killed in traffic accident but in a fight. It was impossible to know exactly what had transpired. One version was that he was attacked by several men in a restaurant in his Navy uniform due to mistaken identity. He got smashed with chairs and was stabbed in his head by a bayonet. He developed seizure and was vomiting. There was a visiting Japanese neurosurgeon at Chợ Rẫy Hospital and Dr. Tùng asked him to help. Hope against hope, an operation was performed to save his life but Fang never regained consciousness and expired two days later.

By tradition, parents would not attend the funeral of a deceased child, and the coffin was sealed up quickly to shun additional misfortunes. I missed the opportunity to see my brother one last time; my wish was kind of coming true for I did not see his disfigured appearance.

Every relative and acquaintance felt sorry for my nineteen year old brother, if not intoxicated he might not be killed for he was a very agile young man.

My parents appeared perceptibly much older after that. A solemn lesson for me was that life was fleeting and unpredictable. What was the meaning of life, born, grew up and then died in a meaningless brawl? Was there justice after death from a sovereign of the netherworld as known in Chinese mythology? Was there really another life after this one?

What puzzled me was the inexplicable telepathy over the distance of 200 plus miles from Saigon to Pleiku. How could my expiring brother produce and transmit such a powerful electromagnetic signal to me hundreds of miles away, without advance notice or applicable device? Looking back, I realized that it was not just another paranormal case of telepathy, but my first wake-up call to the reality of the supernatural from God.

Following the tradition, professionals were hired for the funeral service. In the customary way, the coffin straddled on two wooden saw horses; in front of it was set a table, thereupon were portrait of Ju-Fang, two white candles, joss sticks, a bowl of cooked rice with a pair of chopsticks inserted straight down, a plate of cooked vegetables, three cups of rice wine and three cups of tea. On the ground there was a tin pail for the burning of netherworld moneys. The syncretistic ceremony of Buddhism, Confucianism, and Taoism lasted for an entire evening with dirges accompanied by trumpet, drum and cymbals. One person repeated seven times a ritual of straightening out a tangled rope of karma's knots.

The funeral in the following morning was attended by many relatives and friends.

Meaning of Life and Death

The loss of life was unavoidable but when it struck close to one's heart, it was drastically difficult to bear, and the question about life and death was not philosophical anymore. My pursuit for the answer came to fruition a decade and half later, after going through the valley of the shadow of death more than once.

Life in Pleiku

Pleiku was a remote place yet life in the Medical Group was not rough. To transfer to Saigon was difficult, I had no other place in mind that I would like to transfer to and be able to help out Dad's business. Bachelor soldiers liked to joke: It was easy to come to Pleiku but hard to leave; man would leave with wife and woman with kids (actually, any locale would fit in the jovial quote).

There was not much to do in the military town, so I looked forward to do some part-time study. The University of Saigon's College of Liberal Arts offered correspondence courses; the subject easy for me would be English, so I registered, bought my textbooks and was ready to begin, but I could not manage to sit down and study. A few months later, our BOQ was burned to the ground. My intent to study got a setback then vanished.

Pleiku situated on a plateau 2,480 feet or 756 meters above sea level, combining the fertile volcanic soil with cool climate, it was ideal for the cultivation of tea and coffee, and plantations had been established since the colonial period. Pleiku was strategic in guarding the trilateral borders of Vietnam, Cambodia, and Laos. There were a few major streets, and two national highways Fourteen and Nineteen met at the edge of the town. Highway Nineteen began from the coastal city Qui Nhơn on the east and ended at Pleiku; Highway Fourteen traversed the Central Highlands on a north-south axis.

Pleiku had coffee shops all over the place and were the places where single soldiers frequented. Winter temperatures in the highlands could go down to the thirties at night; occasionally we took hot water baths in the Three Star Hot Bathhouse where Catholic ladies regularly gathered to recite their prayer books.

When I came to Pleiku, the Vietnamization of the war was already under way; there were no more U.S. combat units only military advisors. Present were soldiers from Poland, Iran, Indonesia and Canada under the banner of the International Commission for Supervision and Control or ICSC to oversee the supposedly de-escalation of the War while the Paris peace talk was taking place. There were a few bars remained to cater to the foreign servicemen.

At early evening, in groups of two or three, we parked our Jeep on the knoll of the Diệp Kính Circle to walk around the open air market there with merchandise from the PX. We browsed the stands that displayed their goods on pallets or ponchos and then we headed to dinner or snacks. Lt. Điệu and I bought our paperbacks there.

Dining Routine

In the four years out there, I tried different approaches for meals. At first some of us ate at the diner inside the compound but it shut down a few months later. Sometimes we ate at different home-cooking restaurants in town paying our meals by the month. Occasionally we cooked in the BOQ; when we went to the food markets and young female vendors flirted with us to take them home to cook. For weekday breakfasts I had instant noodles or bread and butter from the open air market. There were always grapefruits displayed on food

Military Life

stands but I did not appreciate its taste by then. On weekends, we went out to eat beef noodles, or Hue noodles with pig feet, or Phnom Penh shrimp-and-pork noodles. The most popular Hue noodle place was "Hue Noodle of the Morgue" which was situated adjacent to the morgue of the civilian Pleiku Hospital. General Nguyễn văn Toàn the II Corps Commander was from Hue and his chauffer used to fetch the General's breakfast there.

Surgery and Long Vacation

After a couple months as the Personnel Officer, my hemorrhoids acted up, I did not want to have the surgery done in the Pleiku Military Hospital next door, also as an excuse so that I could spend time in Saigon. With the C.O.'s permission I went home and had the surgery in Cộng Hòa General Hospital. The operation was done by Surgeon Lt. Col. Phước, the Chief of Neurosurgery, friend of Dr. Tùng. In the French traditional approach, all surgeries followed by an in-patient convalescence period, therefore I stayed a week in the Hospital.

During that time, I met 2nd Lt. Hoàng Tiến Lập of the Regional Force, a Cantonese, in the surgery ward. He was recovering from a grenade wound, walking around with a plastic bag for his stoma after the colostomy. Lập was medically discharged from the ARVN later. We became good friends and see each other quite frequently when I was on furlough. (Prior to the Fall of Saigon, Lập and his parents left Vietnam through an arrangement of the U.S. Embassy, because his elder brother was a nuclear physicist in California. Lập called me up one day soon after we arrived in Connecticut in 1979, he was finishing his accounting degree and hurriedly left me his phone number, and that was the last time I heard from him.)

Since Dr. Tùng had so many friends in the medical circle, he wanted me to stay home for the lunar New Year. Therefore, after one month of sick leave, I went to the Central Clinic with the excuse of minor bleeding, and I got another month to stay in Saigon.

Internal Transfer

By then, General Lữ Lan had been replaced by General Ngô Dzu. It was the period our Medical Group began to take up more authority, therefore a Captain with personnel management specialty from II Corps Headquarters was transferred over to take charge Section One. Upon returning to the Group, I was informed that I had been transferred to the Second Ambulance Company as Supplies Officer. I continued to stay in the BOQ because my new unit was in the same compound.

Ambulance Company

Second Ambulance Company had about forty people including three officers; its head was Maj. Lang, the Medical Group's XO. Maj. Lang did not get double pay, but for sure had been getting grease from the Company. The second-in-command of the Company Lt. Lê Chiểu was one of those old CWOs we met in the Military Medicine School. Lt. Chiểu had been in the military for more than thirty years, at first he joined a private army called Catholic Force which was merged with the ARVN in the 1960s. Chiểu learned his auto mechanic trade since that colonial army time.

Sensing Corruption

Although I was officially in charge of supplies but the system had long been set up so that I never saw reports on fuel or car parts, they were handled by an insider clique. I sat behind my desk to read my American paperbacks and signed inspection tags on fire extinguishers or carbines.

Why corruption was rampant in the ARVN? It was primarily due to low pay. In my final rank as 1st Lt. I got 25,000 piasters per month, roughly equivalent to fifty dollars. A Maj. Gen. without family got 40,000 piasters, i.e. eighty dollars; a wife or a child would get an additional 6,000 to 8,000 piasters each. Besides the salary I also got twenty kilograms of rice each month. When I did not cook in the BOQ, my rice ration was given to an old M.Sgt. in the Finance Section, for he was the first one to ask. Unless there was supplemental income, a soldier or public servant had to live a very frugal life.

Although I did not live extravagantly, Dad knew that my salary was even lower than those who worked for him; therefore, he was very generous to supplement my wages whenever I had need. Through an arrangement with a building-material business in the Pleiku Market called Tam Hưng which became my ATM; I went there and got the cash by signing an IOU. The business owner would be reimbursed when he went to Saigon. Besides, whenever I went home, I would be given money from my parents.

Taste Bud Acidometer

One day, I wandered to the garage where Lt. Chiểu was consulted by a soldier mechanic on the acidity of a new battery; Chiểu poked his index finger into the battery then tasted the electrolyte on his tongue and said that was not sour enough!

Another interesting thing I learned about cars was that instead of putting a 50/50 ratio of antifreeze and water in the radiator, the first thing they did to the newly arrived vehicles was drained the radiator and put in plain water.

Mahjong

The favorite pastimes for officers were mahjong and tennis. Maj. Lang and some of the physicians and pharmacists were addicted to mahjong. On weekends, even some weeknight people gambled through the night. Dad was experienced in mahjong and he did not want his children getting into it, therefore, he did not even allow us to be spectators of the game when we were kids. Dad warned me not to get involved in any gambling, not just mahjong, because gambling and cheating usually went hand in hand. I had never had the opportunity to play mahjong until then. I learned my mahjong faster than all the other greenhorns, for the game pieces were in Chinese. Not until paying my mahjong debt with my five-band Sony radio then I quit for good. Maj. Lang lost much money in his mahjong games, and occasionally he borrowed from me. One day, he had disagreement with me on how much he owed me over time, since he was my superior so I had but agreed to his calculation; then I accompanied him no more to the mahjong table.

Tennis

Tennis had been the sports for the well-to-do. The first tennis court I went to was the one in the Thirty Seventh Artillery Battalion. It was the similar arrangement in my middle school using the court both for basketball and tennis. This cement court was not level for it was constructed upon a slope. I was quite good in table tennis and badminton; it was not that hard for me to switch to tennis. After my initial exposure, on the next trip home I bought a booklet on tennis and studied the basics. I was better off in comparison to the other Medical Service Corps officers financially and athletically, therefore I was the only one that could afford to accompany the doctors, dentists and pharmacists to play tennis.

Tennis Pals

Through playing tennis we met many senior officers and foreigners, such as the Commander of the Thirty Seventh Artillery Battalion Nguyễn Mạnh Tuấn who was later recognized by the ARVN as one of the best unit commanders, and the Commander of Second Calvary, Nguyễn Đức Dung later promoted to full colonel. Col. Dung frequently phoned to

Military Life

my C.O. to take me out to his tennis court by his chauffeur. His tennis court was set up in a hangar of the former Fourth Air Calvary's Camp Holloway. The trip took me all the way from one end of the town to the other. Each time I was riding in the Colonel's Jeep, tanker soldiers wearing black berets saluted the vehicle which was highly polished with two tall antennae and a yellow plate on the front bumper, where usually reserved for the display of a general's stars, painted in English "C.O. 2nd Calvary."

After Col. Dung became the Head of Pleiku Province, he found a 2nd Lt. in the Regional Force that played tennis very well, from then on he stopped seeing me. Whenever we drove past the provincial mansion, Col. Dung was on the tennis court enjoying the game.

When our tennis games got improved, we stopped going to the slanted court instead went to the one in our backyard. This court formerly belonged to the U.S. Advisory Team; it was located inside the II Corps Headquarters compound not far from our Dispensary. There, we met two middle-aged Americans both worked alongside II Corps' G6, i.e. Intelligence. One of the Americans frequently shared with us his Tretorn brand tennis balls, which were a bit heavier but lasted longer on cement surface. This man had very strong serves but once we returned his serves then we would win easily because he could not run. The other guy had a small American car Skylark with automatic shift. I had ridden with him once returning from the court to our unit; it was very noticeable of the downshift clicks when the car climbed uphill. We met also two New Zealand nurses there.

Once we went in the tennis court and saw the Corps Commander and his Chief of Staff playing, we saluted them and left. The assistant head of the Corps' G4 Logistics was a tennis enthusiast. He exchanged my new Wilson 3000 racket with his new Wilson 2000, because its grip was one size too big for his hand, probably gifted by someone, and I dared not say no to a powerful Lt. Col. In the court. We met several VNAF pilots, among them was the Head of Air Support Liaison delivering daily briefing to the Corps, from whom we knew that the NVA forces around Pleiku were found to have anti-aircraft batteries and our pilots were having cold feet.

A physician who also liked to play tennis but not mahjong was Lâm Kỳ Hiệp. Dr. Hiệp first worked in the II Corps Dispensary and was transferred a few miles away to the Mountain Hamlet Training Center where Montagnards were trained to protect their villages. Once he invited me to watch the Center's monthly drill of TOW (tube launched, optically tracked, wire guided) missiles, but I missed out that opportunity. TOW missiles had been proven effective tank-killers in the battle of Kontum in 1972.

Ghost Translator

Physicians were in high demand in the military. They left medical school and clinical residency before graduation, and were inducted to military service with the rank of 1st Lt. (the same rank for pharmacists and dentists).

Normally, physicians graduated after presented theses on clinical studies or medical researches, due to the War a thesis then could be the translation of a chapter from the approved medical textbooks. Doctor Hoàng Xuân Trường asked me to help in translating such a chapter. Another physician Lê Hồng Chí originally had his clinical study data on acupuncture but his manuscript turned to ashes when our BOQ was burned down, he too asked me to help. Therefore, I had been given two copies of doctoral thesis, wherein my name was acknowledged. By then the theses were typewritten and only limited stenciled copies produced, so these were precious memorabilia. My copies were left behind when we withdrew from the Highlands. It would be interesting if I could check back to see how my translations should be improved.

The Promotion Protocol

The first two promotions of CWOs graduated from the OCS were automatic. Counting eighteen months from the date of commissioning, CWO got promoted to 2nd Lt., and the omega was replaced by a golden plum flower. An additional two years then another plum flower would be added on. There were exceptions due to extraordinary merits in the battlefield.

It was a happy occasion for a new rank along with pay increase. For each ceremony of pinning on new rank, there would be a party for all the officers with champagne, provided by the newly promoted.

Trip to Qui Nhơn

Once I was to pick up our new ambulances from Qui Nhơn: six Jeep ambulances refurbished in Okinawa. Since many of our soldiers were from that coastal city they welcomed the assignment. Before our departure a soldier had arranged my stay with his family. The drive down Highway Nineteen was scenic but also somewhat hazardous. Along the 100 or so miles of winding course down to the coast, M113 Armored Personnel Carriers were deployed here and there; the fire bases formerly set up by U.S. forces were still manned along the route. In the vicinity of Qui Nhơn, Korean soldiers were patrolling the highway on foot. With all the presence of our forces on this strategic highway, sniper shots or roadblocks happened sporadically, therefore we all put on our helmets and flak jackets.

Goat Liver

In this trip, the one thing stood out was an invitation to a goat feast in the Qui Nhơn Military Hospital. At the start of the meal as the honor guest I was offered the best part of the goat: a large piece of liver. That organ had the strongest taste I experienced ever. After my cautious nibbling of one small bite, all the following hot pepper, beer, and rice wine could not overcome the taste in my mouth and stomach. I was envious of those soldiers that were enjoying heartily the remainder of the liver, was it a taste that could be acquired? I would not try a second bite.

Vehicular Conversion

After the uneventful trip back to Pleiku, by and by we reshaped the ambulances. By taking away the litter shelves and the extensions, we replaced the tarpaulins with big red crosses with the regular ones. The converted Jeeps were for the many officers joining the Medical Group. Our Ambulance Company used only one or two Dodge ambulances for the occasional support to the II Corps Headquarters.

Dung Beetle Army

For safety's sake, we only drove to places that were not too far out. The furthest place we had ventured out was a Montagnard hamlet name Trung Nghĩa in Kontum Province. When walking down the slope behind the long houses, we saw the entire area covered with dung beetles, as fast as possible, we ran away from the crawling army.

Jackfruit and Montagnard Pig

Pleiku was famous for its jackfruit. The favorite jackfruit was the dry variety, its fleshy part were crispy and filled with nectar. On one occasion we went to a Montagnard hamlet to buy one from the trees. Those huge fruits pulled down the branches almost to the ground weighing thirty some pounds each.

On another occasion, we bought a Montagnard pig and brought it back to Pleiku; I asked the guy on the sidewalk of Diệp Kính Circle selling Cantonese BBQ to roast it for us, and he did it for free. These pigs were relatively small in size, dark in color with bellies almost touching the ground. The young pigs always had triangles made out of bamboos hung on their necks to prevent them poking in the garden fences. These pigs fed on plants and roots, moved around a lot, therefore their meat were lean and very tasty.

War or Peace?

It was 8:00 a.m. Sunday, January 28, 1973, the moment for the long-awaited announcement of the Paris Peace Accord. Our Ambulance Company gathered for the flag raising ceremony and to listen to the Presidential address. Almost right on the dot, we heard the sounds of rocket launching and several rockets landed in front of the II Corps Headquarters where many were also assembled for the historical occasion. Immediately, the Corps called to dispatch an ambulance, a Montagnard Lt. Col. was killed. The war went on when the ink had yet dried, so much so for a peace treaty.

Loss by Fire

One day when I was on furlough, Dr. Lê Hồng Chí came to inform me to bring some clothing on returning to Pleiku, because our barrack was gone. Gone in the fire were my books for the correspondence courses, two medical books in English, and a carbine.

The fire originated from the room occupied by a Signal Corps officer Lt. Lâm Ngọc Trãng in the early morning. Luckily, none of occupants in the BOQ got hurt. Lt. Trãng later on was transferred.

The reason we had a Signal Officer was that he was in charge of communication in the Medevac Center, where we contacted the Directorate of Medical Corps and the Air Force on the airlift of the wounded and sick.

First Roommate

After Lt. Trãng left, Lt. Xuân head of the Medevac Center transferred to the South and the opening was filled by Trần

Khả Lập, a pharmacist. This was an extraordinary arrangement; obviously a pharmacist should never hold such a job.

Lập was involved in the "rebellion" of Dr. Hà Thúc Nhơn at Nguyễn Huệ Military Hospital. The incident started out as a confrontation against corruption in the Board of Medical Discharge. Dr. Nhơn and his in-patient followers occupied part of the Hospital, finally the insubordination was crushed and he was killed. Lập was jailed two years for his role as second-in-command of the "rebellion", and relegated to Pleiku after serving his prison term.

Lập was about six feet tall with dark complexion and played tennis well. He shared my room in the crude cement block barrack built inside the original clubhouse after our BOQ was consumed by fire. On a couple occasions, the two of us practiced tennis on the red-dirt backyard, without net or demarcation. He gave me a good tip: do your best to put the tennis ball back to your opponent's court and let him make the unforced error.

Lập did not have a hard time in the prison, because he was treated as a hero and played tennis with the prison's commandant daily. Lập applied his lab skills in cooking, and taught me some tricks in preparing meals. At nighttime, he listened secretively, inside the mosquito net, broadcasts from Hanoi and the National Liberation Front (NLF); it was quite understandable due to his dissatisfaction with the regime and that he became a Vietcong sympathizer while in jail. Lập transferred back home to Phan Rang at the beginning of 1975. I heard a rumor that Lập became the provincial head of Phan Rang after the Communist takeover. How long could he last in the new regime? Most likely, he would meet the same fate, if not worse, of all those in the NLF that proffered their means and lives to the Communist utopia: in a few years, they had all their power and weapons stripped away.

Military Life

Return to the Medical Group

After spending a year in the Ambulance Company, I returned to the Group to fill the vacancy of Officer of Operations and Training, which was open after Lt. Điệu transferred to his home province of Bình Dương.

A month before the transfer, my replacement in the Ambulance Company came: CWO Khang, a devout Catholic who religiously read his prayer book before retiring. Later, Khang was transferred to the Phú Bổn Sector Hospital because he was one month late on his furlough without justification; CWO Trần Minh Khiếu came to fill the vacancy.

Misunderstandings abound in every society, in addition to prejudices. Even within the officer corps, some wondered jokingly why I served in the military. Because they had ingrained somehow that Chinese could and would always buy their way out from military service.

Lessons in Driving

I was quite unique because of my Chinese descent, English capability, relatively easy on money, and always had a Jeep due to the positions I held. I was the few ones that knew how to drive before joining the Army, and I had given driving lessons to several on the helipad.

I had driven different varieties of Jeep from the WWII vintage (which we called tall Jeep) to M151A1 and M151A2 (short Jeep) with the exception of the Renegade (big belly Jeep) which was solely equipped to the National Police. Driving the M151A2 felt like a powerful and roomy sedan. I once tried out a Dodge ambulance that our unit used as a commuter bus for the soldiers. I drove it on the gravel road around the compound and lost my interest after a hundred feet or so, because the clutch was so stiff.

Once I was showing some newly arrived pharmacists around in a tall Jeep, as I made a left hand turn to the Cù Hanh Market without braking, although the speed was around five mph, the right wheels lifted off the ground, and all the passengers squealed. Those pharmacists would not ask me for a ride anymore. On another occasion, I swung my A1 Jeep into the carport as I had done so many times before; the bumper struck a supporting pole made from angled iron and bent it. Luckily nobody even noticed that the carport had been damaged. With lessons like these, they made me a better driver.

Responsibilities

As the Officer of Operations and Training, I had under me an Officer of Training Lt. Hiệp, two NCOs and three soldiers. We did not do much with the Operations part because medical support activities in Military Region Two were well taken care of by our organic units. Primarily we focused on the corpsman training in our compound. We had training courses for basic medics year round, each lasted for eight weeks; the soldiers came from all branches of the Army including Women's Auxiliary Corps. After successfully completing the course the soldiers returned to their units to serve in the new capacity as corpsmen or nursing aides; they would get stipends in addition to their salaries. There was an officer served as the Commander of the Trainee Company and a NCO assistant to supervise the trainees, whom were assigned to occasional details.

War Casualty

One afternoon, there were two rockets flew overhead towards the air base, we ran for cover to an aboveground bunker. It was not the first time we were under attack, but this round the trajectory was so low and the rocket landed on our perimeter, therefore the roar was very loud. At that moment I was running on the gravels my left leg slipped, I fell down and scraped off some skin on my knee, I stood up at once and got into the bunker. From then on, a joke circulated in the unit that Lt. Quốc was scared to death by a rocket flying overhead.

In that rocket attack, a medic trainee was killed. He was clearing weeds by the roadside; a piece of shrapnel from the rocket explosion severed a blood vessel in his chest while no one nearby got hurt. A life got snatched away just like that! As head of the S3, I was the number four person in the unit. When the X.O. was on leave for more than a week, I would take up his task to read and assign documents received.

Medical Bookcase

When the MACV Medical Advisors were departing, they gave our Group dozens of medical textbooks and related materials. I was ordered to catalog and shelf them in the glass-enclosed medicine cabinet situated in the CO's office.

Boot Sizes

When the Advisors were there, I talked to them once a while. One thing that caught my attention was that a young GI of my height wore boots three sizes bigger than mine. Our boots were made in the U.S. without any distinction of width yet they fit well; now in the States the shoes could not fit me comfortably unless they were marked "wide", and my shoe size rose from six to eight and half.

Opportunities Stolen

I had two opportunities to have my military career switched to a different direction and stationing in Saigon but got stopped cold. In early 1974, the Medical Corps wanted to send somebody to attend the Language School at Lackland Air Base in San Antonio, Texas. The eligibility was an officer of the Medical Corps (including the Medical Service Corps) who scored top in an English test. After finishing the training, the officer was to teach conversational English in the Military Medicine School. I grabbed the opportunities and took the test. With help from Lt. Lương Tô, one of the many English instructors of Chinese descent in the ARVN Language School,

I borrowed tapes from him and got myself familiarized with the contents and the announcer's tone.

Among the applicants were doctors, pharmacists, and I was the only Administrative Officer. I got the highest score of 93/100 but a pharmacist was chosen. By the year's end, another opening was up, and I was on the top again with an even higher score of 97/100. Per Lt. Tô, my score was higher than most of the instructors who had completed the training course in Texas. This round a physician was chosen and I was listed on the official notification as replacement in case the first pick could not go. Twice in a row, my absolute certainty of going to the U.S., after the missed opportunity in the OCS, had been frustrated by some power play. Many things in this world would not happen the way that was supposed to!

A Passing Comment

After the last furlough of the year I went back to Pleiku before Christmas. In my customary way of going on leaves at least four times a year, I was already planning to request the next one on March 15, 1975.

One day, my NCO of Operation, S.Sgt. Thái Nhân An told me: "Lieutenant, there is a new cashier in Café Thảo; she's very pretty, go and court her! Don't be disappointed too quickly though, at first sight she looks like a handsome guy." I said, "Fine, I'll be there."

Sgt. An confided to me that he was to go AWOL on his coming furlough. He would go to Phnom Penh to get away from this drawn-out war for good. He asked me to take care of his belongings and send them back to his parents in Cholon. Sgt. An had been a good guy except having a loud mouth after drinking. I wished him well. As had been planned he did not show up as required. Personnel Section reported his AWOL and listed him as a deserter. A couple months later, when I was ready to send out his belongings, all the roads to Saigon had been cut off.

For years, my efforts to find Thái Nhân An turned up nothing; I was afraid that he had perished in the killing fields of the ruthless Khmer Rouge. Finally, after forty one years I bumped into his email address in a Free Pacific Language Institute alumni website; he was alive and well in California. By providence An left Phnom Penh two weeks before its collapse.

Meeting My Better Half
One evening, a few of us went to the café. When it was time to leave I volunteered to pay at the counter to take a look at the cashier. What Sgt. An had said was very true; by a quick glance the cashier with a demi-garçon haircut could easily be passed up as a handsome lad. I hesitated to strike up a conversation for there must be many guys already courting such a beautiful girl, and it made no sense to get in queue.

A couple days later, I went to see pharmacist Lâm văn Sử my classmate in Pharmacy School. He and another guy rented a room in the city instead of living in the Medical Group's compound, and the cashier girl was there along with Sử's girlfriend. I was struck dumb to see her under broad daylight. She was so pretty! Her name was Nga. The one thing impressed me most was that she wore no makeup, no perfume, and no jewelry. She just quit her job at the café, due to the threats from some customers who tried unsuccessfully to ask her out. Nga came from Ban Me Thuột not too long ago and she was staying with a relative in the Air Base.

We got acquainted and went together to eat, see places such as Biển Hồ (Lake of Sea), watch the movie "Mayerling" by Catherine Deneuve and Omar Sharif. We went to the Fairy Creek adjacent to the Montagnard Training Center and Dr. Lâm Kỳ Hiệp took many pictures of us. (None of the photos survived the calamitous withdrawal. The whereabouts of Dr. Hiệp after April 30, 1975 remained unknown till this day.)

Nga, or Anna her baptismal name, took me to attend a Catholic Mass in the center of town. The church was not big and filled from wall-to-wall on Sunday; we only got to stand outside the church door.

Everything happened so fast, we fell in love fervently and I proposed to her.

According to military regulations, in order to wed to an officer, the fiancée must first obtain security clearance. In addition to that Anna was a Roman Catholic, I had to become a Catholic, and announcements of marriage be read in Masses for six months in her home diocese then the priest would legitimately perform the sacrament of matrimony; not to mention I got to have the blessings from her parents as well as mine. I planned to go on leave on March 12, so I could bring her home to meet my parents and see her parents as well. When preparing to file my marriage application then I realized that Anna also bore the family name of Trần!

Anna was a good cook and very speedy in food preparation; she kept our living quarters clean and tidy. Once a while, we invited Lt. Hiệp, Officer of Training, over for dinner. For some reason, her stay inside the compound raised no concern from Security or they were so used to the month-long stays of fiancées or wives of other officers. I had thought of moving out of the compound to the city but was not in a hurry to do so.

A Sudden Twist

As our Medical Group had taken up more responsibility the Joint General of Staff notified us that a high-echelon delegation would come to inspect at the end of March, the C.O. ordered S3 to prepare a mock-up inspection put things in tiptop shape for the visit. O my, my preplanned furlough had to be put on hold and not to purchase Air Vietnam tickets leaving on March 12!

Chapter 4.

Prisoner of War and "Reeducation"

After Route Nineteen—the artery connecting Pleiku to the eastern coast had been cut off for a couple days; Ban Mê Thuột on our south connecting through Route Fourteen was overrun by the NVA on March 10.

The situation was getting more serious day by day. Air Vietnam stopped the service linking Saigon and Pleiku on the twelfth; even if I had bought tickets for that date beforehand, we would be stuck nonetheless.

Retreat from the Highlands

On March 15, President Thiệu met with II Corps Commander Maj. Gen. Phạm văn Phú in Cam Ranh Bay and ordered the establishment of a Forward Command in Nha Trang to take back Ban Mê Thuột, all available forces of the Corps would redeploy to Nha Trang immediately. Pleiku was in turmoil, a hundred thousand soldiers were to uproot from the strategic Central Highlands, in a hurry and without planning!

Through the night, many rockets roared over our heads hitting the air base. I knew many officers and soldiers among us were storming the air base to board the outgoing flights. In the air base I knew only three OCS classmates in the MP and K9 units; even if Anna and I managed to get through the base entrance which was fifty yards from our gate, I had no confidence that we could fight against the crowd to get on a plane.

It was early Sunday morning, March 16, 1975. After an evening of mad dash, our trucks were lined up between the gate and the Command Post. Soldiers and their families were scrambling around the compound packing up for the withdrawal. I took a quick nap after an exhaustive night of last-minute preparation, expected a tough day lying ahead. In his office, Surgeon Lt. Col. Phạm Gia Tự told me to meet him at the II Corps Tactical Operation Center for further instructions on the retreat. Besides the C.O. I was the highest ranking officer.

About 6:30 a.m. I walked up the barrack where my M151A2 Jeep was parked with everything needed for the journey. I got into the Jeep; Anna sat next to me on a wooden plank spanning the front seats on top of the gear box. On the passenger side was my Officer of Training 2nd Lt. Hiệp, holding an M-16 rifle, sharing his seat was a medic trainee from the Rangers holding an M79 grenade launcher, he was drafted by 2nd Lt. Phạm Quốc Thoại Trainee Company Commander as our bodyguard. In the back, besides Lt. Thoại there were three 1st Lt. Pharmacists reported to duty only a week ago awaiting unit assignment; the three had been in the air base during the night and could not get on the outbound flights. They showed up at the last minute in my living quarters to get a ride. At first, I had the Jeep's rear compartment for the family of my subordinate Corporal Chung Đức Hiệp, his wife, and four young children. The unexpected appearance of the pharmacists was a tough decision for me; finally I had to remove Hiệp's family and asked them to go to the GMC trucks, which were already filled with people and belongings.

Driving down the gravel road to the headquarters, people were bustling between the barracks and the trucks, squeezed their belongings into the vehicles. Dozens of trucks, ambulances and Jeeps with engines running hummed like a busy bus terminal. A soldier ran away from the generator followed by an explosion that detonated beneath it. Everybody knew that it was a no-return trip so they did not want anything useful left behind for the enemy. I stepped into the C.O.'s office. A small fire had just started on a pile of binders, documents, and medical books; an M-72 Light Anti-tank Weapon was laid on top of the heap. I had no use for the rocket, but I did not want it to go off changing the Quonset hut into a huge fragmentary bomb when our people might still be around, so I stomped out the fire.

I drove to the head of the column of vehicles and turned left to the side entrance of the II Corps Headquarters, the small convoy followed after our Jeep. The sentry station had been deserted. Driving past our II Corps Dispensary, I saw a couple soldiers walking quietly on the roadside. I stopped at the front of the Tactical Operation Center and saw nobody around, even the front gate was half-closed. I got off the Jeep and walked towards the Center. Suddenly I heard the noise of an approaching helicopter; I turned around and saw it landed about twenty yards away on a helipad. Dr. Tự got out of the chopper and came to me. Very briefly, he told me that he was flying to Nha Trang, there was an unoccupied seat and I could go with him. I entertained the tempting thought for a split second, and declined his kind offer. I presumed that it would be futile to ask for an additional seat for my newlywed; the one thing I was certain was that I would not go by myself without her, or send her off alone. He shook my hand and gave me the last order: "Lieutenant Quốc, now I put the Unit under your command. I'll meet you in Nha Trang."

Warning Shots

I saluted. He turned and boarded the helicopter. As I looked on, it ascended and flew southeastwards.

At that moment, I was overwhelmed. It was a weird yet despondent feeling. I realized that we were plunging headlong into a twilight zone on our own. We were armed but not combat-ready; we had families coming along on a retreat route with no plan, no coordination, and no commander. Strangely, I recalled the last combat lesson from the OCS: "The Company on Retreat." The lesson stated emphatically that it was a last-ditch effort, demanded the utmost in planning, courage and sacrifice. The lesson never anticipated a withdrawal along with family or personal belongings. I did not want to be a hero leading the unit to safety and get a promotion or a medal for that matter, but at this moment of no return, I did not really make the choice, the lot was cast.

Years later, some people judged that I was stupid not to beg my C.O. and he might squeeze out an extra seat for Anna, then we would fly to Nha Trang comfortably without enduring the needless ordeal. Since I was alive, was my decision unwise? It made no difference now. All I knew was that in the ensuing saga both of us had been well taken care of by the Almighty whom we were yet to know. What happened from then on was a chain of events impossible to comprehend.

I led the convoy reversing the route we came in. When we were passing by our barracks I took a deep hard look at the BOQ and the compound. I tried to absorb everything into my mind. This was the first and only military post where I spent four and half years, the prime of my life. I murmured farewell and my eyes fogged up. I noticed that Anna was surveying the shack that had been called home for a month and half.

When we made the turn at the gate of the air base, it was wide open and no MPs were in sight.

Our column of vehicles went by the places that were so familiar to us: the Cù Hanh Market, II Corps Maternity Ward, the Pleiku Civilian Hospital, the Provincial Headquarters, and Diệp Kính Cinema. At Diệp Kính Circle we turned left towards Route Fourteen. We drove by the open air market, Air Vietnam, and Thần Phong Market. After the Thanh An junction where National Highways Fourteen and Nineteen intersected, I bore to the southeast onto Provincial Route 7B. The secretive cover had been blown away. A hundred thousand people rushed onto a two-lane country road, vehicles of all descriptions joined the convoy which later known as the "Convoy of Tears".

Provincial Route 7B was in disuse for decades, it had been mined by the Tiger Division of South Korea, and the bridge crossing the River Ba had long gone; for the retreat, the Seventh Combat Engineer Group was ordered to build a pontoon bridge there. When the withdrawal was known, the NVA marched from Ban Mê Thuột to join hands with the local Vietcong forces to intercept us.

Phú Bổn Province situated in a valley, the provincial route started with a hilarious hairpin turn. In the afternoon we came to Phú Bổn Sector Hospital in the provincial seat known as Hậu Bổn or Cheo Reo.

Lt. Khang, my former replacement at the Second Ambulance Company, led Anna and me to the officers' dormitory to rest for the night; he said that the Colonel Provincial Chief ordered everyone to stay put while the road to the coast was being cleared.

Corporal Hiệp came to inquire about his family members; I could not answer him because they boarded different vehicles and most of our trucks rushed on after a short stop at the hospital. Hiệp was crestfallen and I was sorry for not able to help him at all.

Lt. Hoàng from the Second Field Hospital came to see me pleaded for five gallons of gasoline; I had to decline for I had only that much reserved for my Jeep, besides I had no idea where our gas supplies were. Lt. Hoàng was lucky to have come down from Kontum, for the Colonel Provincial

Chief of Kontum was killed by sniper fire on Route Fourteen before reaching Pleiku.

A Road Stuck

Next morning, the seventeenth of March, with the same group of people, our Jeep moved out from the Hospital and came to a standstill about three miles down the road. We walked around to assess the situation and found everything topsy-turvy.

Our Ranger medic trainee fetched water and cooked rice in his helmet. My acquaintances that owned the Tam Hưng building materials were nearby also preparing their meals. We exchanged some niceties and parted our way. Hiệp and Thoại asked if I could lend them insignias of 1st Lt. in order to command more authority from other troops, but I did not have any. Somehow Thoại managed to obtain one and pin it on his chest. By nightfall we spread out the ponchos and slept on the paved road.

The next day March 18, we inched up a little bit and went by a burnt military fuel truck underneath was a charred body. Sporadic gunfire aggravated our concerns. A bloody and moaning Ranger was carried down the hill by two buddies on a blood-stained hammock tied to a tree limb.

To Risk or Not

There was a detachment of Rangers and some M-48 tanks nearby, we approached them and saw several officers studying a map spread on the ground. One of the pharmacists bumped into his friend, the physician of the tank company.

The troops decided to use the tanks to rush through the stranglehold by positioning Rangers on the outside of the tanks to suppress enemy fires. By the request of the tank unit physician, our Medical Group officers were approved to sit alongside with the Rangers. I did not want to do that for it was physically demanding and too risky. Therefore, we two stayed behind; the three pharmacists, Hiệp, Thoại, and the medic trainee departed with the tanks. In April, one of the pharmacists came back to Saigon and visited my family; he got a broken arm after brushing off the tank by a tree limb.

Missing In Action

Thirty five years later, in August of 2010, after numerous searches on the Internet I found Thoại, now a renowned Vietnamese author in Winnipeg, Canada. He said that in the Medical Group roll call in Nha Trang, only Corporal Dương Thái Sanh and I were absent; everybody felt sorry for the two MIAs. It was a great surprise for him that Anna and I had survived. We exchanged long phone conversations to fill in the big gap of thirty five years. Thoại sent me his article about his Route 7B adventure. I felt much better in learning that Corporal Hiệp had reunited with his family.

Convoy of Tears

I heard that Colonel Phạm văn Tất Commander of II Corps Rangers had been promoted to Brigadier General and was put in charge of the withdrawal, but the convoy was in disarray, even units that were able to hang on together struggled for their own survival.

At the evening, we were told that an M113 Armored Personnel Carrier ahead of us had some rooms; when Anna and I were rushing towards the APC suddenly we heard an explosion inside of it and some people ran out. In confusion, we got back to our Jeep.

That night, the road was solidly packed and no room for us to lie down as in the previous evening. In order to sleep, Anna curled up in the Jeep. I tried not to lie on the hood but really need to have some rest, so I climbed to the top of the Jeep and balance myself on the three supporting tube frames. It was quite scary and very uncomfortable. I tossed and turned with extreme care and eventually got some sleep by performing the acrobatics.

Unplanned Encounter

I woke up in my half-soaked uniform from the morning dews. Looking around I found Lương văn Bác who was a soldier in my S3 for a while, then he went to the OCS and was assigned to the Regional Force after graduation, now a platoon leader with the rank of 2nd Lt. His unit stationed somewhere between Kontum and Pleiku, he ran away after hearing about the retreat and got there by himself. I welcomed him to our group and I did not mind having an old buddy who had seen real action.

Convoy Attacked

In the mid-morning, an Air Force GMC truck in front of us suddenly fired its .50 caliber machine gun to the rear of us. I looked and to my absolute horror a group of Vietcong in black pajamas were running and shooting at the convoy column. Bursts of gunshot mingled with the explosions of grenades and RPG drove everyone to seek cover. Bác told us to take shelter in a cluster of bananas on the roadside for protection. Quickly we hid in the banana bush and the fighting was getting more intense with people shrieking and crying all around us. I checked around and decided to leave the area and go toward the foothill behind the adjacent rice paddies. Without much thinking I followed the advice that if you carry no weapon and wear no uniform then you would not become a shooting target, I left everything in the bush including my knapsack, rifle, and jacket. I grabbed a canteen and a bag of pre-cooked rice.

Wandering in the Wood

We rushed through the paddy as many were also fleeing the scene of fighting. The two of us were on our own from that point on.

March was hot and dry, under stress people got very thirsty and streams were nowhere near the road. We saw a lone young boy eight or nine years old drinking the muddy water he scooped up from the rice paddy with a helmet. I was wondering the boy would get dysentery and devastated from it later.

Without maps or compass, I aimed east to the direction of the coast which was at least sixty miles away. The paddies ended by the edge of the forest, it was very tranquil after the distance we had covered. Once in a while we bumped into other small bands of wandering soldiers. From one of these folks I learned to pick the leaves from some vines looked like bougainvillea which brought some relief to the thirsty mouth with the limey salivating taste. They also gave us advice not to drink water in big gulps, not only it would exhaust our water fast but also could not quench the thirst; the right way to drink from the canteen was to pour water into its cap and take one capful at a time.

Bliss & Troubles

I was wondering why Anna was drinking so much water then she told me that she was in the family way!

Since Anna did not have means for proper personal hygiene for three days; physiological changes of the pregnancy led to leucorrhoea, and the discharges soaked her panty. We left everything behind in the Jeep or in the knapsack, she got no extra underwear. The only solution was to give her mine! We found a secluded place and I gave her my Jockey brief.

Jacket from Heaven

On my upper body all I had was a green collared T-shirt and the temperature was dropping. A group of five or six soldiers appeared and I struck up a conversation with their leader 1st Lt. Nguyễn văn Định, an artillery battery commander of the Twenty Third Army Division. They pulled out from their position when they got the news of the withdrawal and left the four big guns behind. He noticed that I did not even have my full fatigues on, told a soldier that happened to have an extra field jacket in the knapsack to give it to me.

Finally, an armed band of soldiers led by Maj. Bảo Đồng from II Corps G4 joined in. Although we had nothing to discuss but we stayed close together for it was getting dark fast. Anna and I shared half bag of the rice with water. Nightfall descended like a thick curtain, I raised my hand in front of me and could not see it.

Last Day of Freedom

We spent the night half reclining on the gentle slope of a ravine; I was exhausted and fell asleep in no time. I woke up by some murmuring sounds from people realizing that the small group under Maj. Đồng had sneaked away during the night. With such a mixed group of soldiers and families like ours that could go nowhere, anyone with a right mind and being certain that he could find the way out would do so. I looked to the distant ridge where the convoy stood still as the day before. We moved on ourselves. We only had one third of a canteen of water and half a bag of rice.

The two of us walked and walked, and returned to the same spot. We saw a family with several young children, the father lugging on his shoulder a five-gallon plastic container half filled with water which could be good for the family for a few days.

Enemy Territory

On the ground I noticed a wire running along the trail; it was a field telephone line. We are in enemy controlled territory! Quietly, I kept it to myself.

Prisoner of War and "Reeducation"

The two of us spent the morning walking in the forest, we finished the rice and I gave all the water to Anna; I kept my thirst at bay by sucking the sour leaves found here and there. It was in the afternoon, we heard water running, by followed the sound and saw a creek. Gleefully Anna leapt into the shallow stream, scooping up water with her hands and drank heartily. Wading a few steps into the refreshingly cool brook I put in the canteen to fill it up.

Captured by the Enemy

Out of the blue, two warning shots from an AK-47 like thunder claps, the echo combined with the flapping of leaves likened to a flock of frightened birds fluttering for safety, it was extremely startling.

A voice belched out four Vietnamese words: "Surrender live. Resist die!" Hairs stood up on the back of my neck. I saw two soldiers in North Vietnamese Army uniforms standing behind the bushes on the stream's bank pointing their AK-47s at us.

Anna was so frightened, she ran and lost her sabots in the creek; I raced after and grabbed her from behind to calm her down. One soldier yelled at us to come to them. I raised my hands as told and we waded ashore.

Once we stepped on the bank, I was ordered to unlace my boots; bending down I sneakily unbuckled the wristband and let my Omega watch slid down beneath the bush and used my left boot covered it with dirt intended not to let them to have my expensive watch. They apparently saw what I did but said nothing. After removing my boots, one man told me to take off my pants, I was quite hesitant to do that but I had to obey; when they saw my naked butt, they laughed and told me to pull the pants up. One of them came behind me using the bootlaces tied my upper arms tightly. Up close I saw the soldiers were in their late teens.

Warning Shots

We were led a short distance from the creek to a small opening in the trees, where several other POWs were sitting on the jungle floor. A soldier took my wallet and checked my IDs and "realized" that I was a Doc and called me so. The interrogator took away my glasses and wallet with 50,000 piasters, equivalent to 100 dollars. Wearing spectacles were considered impolite, prescription glasses included; therefore, POWs had no right to hold on to them. A week later, they returned my glasses.

A soldier announced that the "Counterfeit Army" had been defeated and was on the run; they had just captured a senior office Lt. Col. Nguyễn Mạnh Tuấn, the Commander of the Thirty Seventh Artillery Battalion.

Not far from us, an ARVN officer was lying on the grass groaning due to stomachache and his friend was comforting him nearby; they were not yelled at but patiently looked on by our captors. While I was awaiting bad things that would happen to us, overheard was a conversation between two NVA soldiers from a short distance away. One asked if he could borrow ten bullets and the answer from the other was negative, for he got only a few left.

Then they separated Anna from me. I remembered that she had lost her footwear in the creek, so I took off my socks and handed them to her. As a young soldier led Anna away, she turned to look at me time after time while I followed her with my blurry unspectacled eyes until she disappeared behind the trees. I thought that it would be the last time seeing her.

Hot Dinner

We were led to a spot corralled with some ropes; therein about twenty ARVN soldiers were sitting. I looked around and found Lt. Định and his men. It was eerily quiet; we were waiting for the fateful things to befall us.

After a while, two POWs walked towards the corral carrying two bags formed from ponchos. I smelled cooked rice, it was dinner! What a relief because I had not eaten much in two days. Each one of us was handed some rock salt, I plucked a leaf to hold them. Then each got a rice ball, which was still warm! It was unheard of in human history that POWs got fed twice in a day even from the very beginning!

Darkness crept in and we slept on the forest floor. I curled on the ground using my elbows alternatively as pillow through the night. I could not imagine if I did not have the jacket which Định ordered his soldier to hand over. I woke up during the night and saw a pair of socks hung drying on a twig next to me; sneakily I took the socks and put them on. The next morning, a neighbor asked around for his socks. He cursed the thief. Since everyone was wearing the same socks, the victim could not tell who the thief was.

The captors needed some porters and would reward the volunteers with something to eat. I volunteered so that might get to see Anna besides food. Most of the POWs went. Under armed guards, each of us was assigned to carry some ammunition, I got two anti-tank mines, and each weighed about thirty pounds, which were strapped onto a snarled tree limb. I tried my best to handle the dangling weights by switching between shoulders. The branch was hurting so much; I struggled to locate the least hurting spot. A guard noticed my awkwardness and cried out: "Lo, the big head guy there! He can't even handle such a tiny load."

Straining my eyes to look around I was unable to spot any civilian. After finishing the task, each POW got a piece of Chinese snack, the NVA called them "dried food", it turned out to be yunpiangao—a sweetened layer cake made of glutinous rice flour flavored with citrus peel. Strewn about in the forest were empty cans in camouflaged paints with white Chinese characters such as white sugar or powdered milk.

In the afternoon, we were herded to the stream to get water and wash ourselves. We were permitted to go out to relieve ourselves not too far away. Besides the excitement of the two meals, we all sat quietly. I could not recall what had gone through my mind during that time, probably self-pity plus worries for Anna. Besides the occasional, far away sound of warfare, we had nothing to do but look at trees and shunning our expressionless faces. We were not allowed to lie down during daytime.

Bidding Farewell

Early next morning, suddenly there was a small commotion in the corral. A woman escorted by a soldier was approaching, and it was Anna! The detained civilians were let go and she came to say good-bye. We looked at each other deeply in the precious moments. I reminded her of my home address in case she could go and see my family. She told me that the captors returned the money. Since 50,000 piasters was an astronomical sum for them, the one who counted the money was either not able to handle the task or keep some for himself, so Anna got only what were handed to her. They also returned her my Omega watch that I tried to bury in the sandbank. I told Anna to take good care of herself and the baby. We hugged each other gently; she walked away and kept looking back until vanishing from my sight. One guy whispered that it was such a heart-wrenching scene. I did not even shed a tear; I was numb.

Relocation

Later that day, we were ordered to move. We formed a single file and were ordered to tie our wrists to a long rope; but we just held it with our hands. Everyone carried his belongings while all I had was the canteen. We walked through the wood and a couple of hills; going up and down the slopes strewn with rocks were hard on my feet. Later on at home and in the "reeducation" camps my feet kept swelling up, probably had something to do with this trek.

During a climb, I raised the canteen to drink and the cap fell off from the connecting band and bounced down the hill. It was a disaster; from then on I had to improvise some stopgap measures to keep in the water.

On the slope there was a set of bleached antlers which one guy asked permission to pick up and carry on his shoulder. After five or ten minutes, our pal gave up and dumped the horns.

After a few hours we came to an opening with lots of captured soldiers milling around, and were ordered to hunker down. I looked around, not that far away there was a small pile of cornmeal on the ground. I thought: should I ask a guard to allow me to scoop them up?

Officer POWs

A NVA soldier came separating the officers from the soldiers, and then the officers moved on. We climbed up a gentle incline and came to some kind of an entrance between two trees. The place was surrounded by a few barbed wires nailed to the trees. Near the gate, an ARVN officer still with his full colonel insignia was standing there observing the newcomers. I had an urge to salute him but stopped short because nobody in front of me did. We had never been taught how to behave as a POW, but I remembered the movie "The Bridge on the River Kwai" wherein the British POWs retained military discipline under their own officers in the prison camp. Here were we, all officers and no one saluted to a colonel.

(After becoming a Christian, I knew that I came out this ordeal alive was all by grace. Reading Vietnam War history, I realized more fully how fragile my situation was. The ARVN was outnumbered and outgunned after the Paris Peace Treaty. From the Central Highlands 50,000 soldiers were ordered to withdraw; the hasty retreat necessarily turned into "The

Convoy of Tears." By estimate, out of the combined total of military and civilian of 100,000-plus, half of them vanished on Provincial Route 7B. I had been kept away from seeing the carnage during my imprisonment, but Anna witnessed horrified scenes on the way home after her release as well as on trips to locate me; her experience might have contributed to the onset of her severe depression five years later. If the NVA was acting even somewhat resembling to the Khmer Rouge, the Red Army, or the Imperial Army of Japan, I was a goner.)

An Unyielding Colonel

The Colonel who insisted on keeping his military insignia was formerly a member of the Bilateral Military Council in representing the Republic of Vietnam to interact with the National Liberation Front, therefore he and his staff could travel safely in the NLF-controlled zones; with such a diplomatic status, the Colonel was protesting his unlawful detention.

In the corral, those of us with similar ranks gathered in makeshift sheds with twigs that we inserted into the ground, the canopies were made out of branches and leaves yanked from trees and shrubs. I found a big and smooth piece of rock, which was my stool during the day, and cold, hard pillow at night.

A Bloody Latrine

A latrine had already been dug at one end of the corral, when needed to release ourselves we had to stand in attention at its entrance and asked permission out loud to step out. A guard was stationing somewhere high up, the first time I ventured out with nobody informing me about the "protocol", I was yelled at and warned that I would be shot the next time.

The latrine was a large rectangular pit with two tree trunks lying across and could hold several men at the same time. I noticed that my hemorrhoids were acting up and lots of blood came out in every bowel movement. Somebody wondered that there was a poor guy bleeding in the latrine like a woman in her period! Occasional sprinkles of spring came down at night, we sat up and waited till the rain halted, then tried to lie down on the damp ground with our damp clothes. We were allowed to build small fires to keep warm and on one occasion we were ordered to stamp out the fires quickly because a VNAF reconnaissance plane was flying over.

Unforgettable Dream

One night I had a dream: I was in a familiar coffee shop of my childhood years and had a very large bowl of noodle soup with cubes of meat floating in it, before taking any to my mouth I was woken with a hurting empty stomach. (It shall even be as when a hungry man dreameth, and, behold, he eateth; but he awaketh, and his soul is empty. Isaiah 29:8b)

I met a 2nd Lt. from the Second Field Hospital in Kontum also a dropout of the Pharmacy School, and had a few exchanges with the doctors from the Twenty Third Medical Battalion.

Every morning, I saw the Colonel doing his calisthenics, which appeared peculiar to me because the movements were performed on one spot. Later on in a "reeducation" camp in Long-Khánh I saw a buddy doing the same exercise and learned that it was the American military calisthenics.

Captured General

One day, there was a commotion in the corral when some POWs arrived. The Colonel went to greet them at the gate, one of whom was Brig. Gen. Trần văn Cầm, Deputy for Tactical Operations of II Corps. He was captured in the Tuy Hòa airfield when his helicopter landed without realizing the NVAs had already overrun it.

Later on that day, my friend from the Second Field Hospital came and showed me happily a five hundred piaster banknote he got from the General whom he acquainted through playing tennis.

Relocations

A couple days later, a military truck came and all POWs above the rank of Major were sent to the North.

Soon afterwards it was our turn to relocate. This time we were going downhill. We went by several spots that M-16 rifles and M-1 carbines were stacked like firewood. Some armed Montagnards walked passed us in opposite direction, they did not pay much attention to us probably had already seen enough of POWs. I saw a single yellowish orange dangling on a tree near the trail, what a torturing scene, but I comforted myself as the fox in Aesop's Fables that failed to reach the grapes—that orange must be very sour otherwise it would not have remained there.

The jungle had many pines which brought up my fatalistic pessimism. I recalled a stanza by a famous Vietnamese poet Nguyễn Công Trứ (1778 -1858):

"Reincarnate not as human next round,
Be a pine aloft makes murmuring sounds."

Finally we came to a former ARVN Regional Force compound known as Camp Hoàng Hoa Thám. It was approximately 120' x 150' with tin roof sheds built along two flanks and several earthen fortifications in between. The earthen fortifications were former machine gun nests with three quarters below ground. The compound was gutted and the sides of the sheds were enclosed by corrugated tins.

After a roll call and the announcement of rules for the new place, we were dismissed. I tried to invite myself to the group of Lt. Định, whom had occupied one of the dugouts, but it was fully occupied so I could not stay.

An Old Friend

I was ready to leave and some people were also coming down to check out the place and surprisingly one of them was 1st Lt. Lê Chiểu of the Second Ambulance Company. I wondered why, since he was no more in the military; he said that although he was in civilian clothing but got detained due to his discharge document.

Although we stayed in the same compound I did not recall if we had any further contact afterwards. Chiểu was short and dark but very tough; there was no problem for him to survive the ordeal. On the other hand, he would assume me a goner after what happened to me later on.

I met a captured Filipino and talked to him briefly in English. He was a contractor mechanic for the M-48 tanks.

Finally, I settled myself in one of the long sheds. We slept on the cement floor, and naturally formed two rows with a passage way between our feet. Each of us had a space about three to four feet wide.

Filming & Trading

We were gathered to wash ourselves in a stream nearby by going through the rear exit. On the way out, a cameraman was aiming his movie camera at us; it was possible that the few frames of me in the POW column would exist in the NVA archive.

We bathed and washed our clothing and fill up our water containers which varied from an aluminum teapot, the plastic covers of flak jackets, even the head from a doll. On the way in, a large crowd of Montagnards with baskets on their backs, gathered along the barbed wire fence and sold us foodstuff. People had money bought green papayas and corns, and the guards did not interfere with the trading.

Rice Ration

The compound held about 200 POWs. Morning and evening there were roll calls and brief admonition; then we were free to roam. We were put in units of ten and each unit received a rice ration. Twice a day, at noon and evening each unit got an aluminum basin with approximately twenty small bowls of cooked rice. Along with the rice were rock salts, sometimes a tiny amount of cooked vegetable from cans, or broth with pork! The broth was made from canned pork from China, with a small lump of fatty pork the size of a fingertip. The meat was mashed and stirred evenly in the broth before distributing to ten containers of different sizes and shapes. I could not recall what I used as container to hold the rice and soup, but disposable chopsticks from twigs were plenteous.

Shaving

One day we were ordered to shave off our mustaches and beards. So we looked for available means to do that. On the ground there were plenty metal straps from ammo boxes, I picked out a piece and sharpened it on the cement floor making it into a crude tweezers to plug out my facial hairs.

Chinese Friend

Among the POWs I found a Chinese guy, 2nd Lt. Hàn Thọ Tường of the Artillery. He attended Saint John's Chinese High School, the sister school of Free Pacific Language Institute. He was a few years my junior but we had some friends in common to talk about.

Odd Interview

One afternoon, I was called to go outside, there sat behind the table a cadre who could speak Putonghua quite well. He told me that his army had taken over the area of Phú Bổn and he could use my help in case they need to talk to the Chinese population out there. But the occasion never arose. How did they find out that I was Chinese? My name would not show that; might it be from my facial feature, but Lt. Tường was not asked.

Got Sick

Three four days later, I got a fever then broke out in diarrhea and lost my appetite. I thought I got a bad cold due to exposure to the elements and the primitive living condition. Trying to avoid the cold water, I did not take the daily bathing in the stream and asked help to have my canteen filled up, although the water might be causing the diarrhea, but what else could I drink? Some people got the means to boil water but those were not my friends.

And Sicker

Every day, I had to leave the shed several times due to diarrhea. There was no problem during daytime, all I needed was requesting permission from the guard, but at night no one was allowed to leave the shed. So when needed to relieve myself I sneaked out to the entrance of the shed in total darkness and did it right there, then covered it up with some dirt. There were no tools to dig up a hole near the entrance or some brooms to gather enough dirt to cover my excrements, so the accumulated foul smell caused complaints in the shed.

I got so sick and was exempted from roll calls. Since I did not wash myself or clothes, the excrement and blood soiled my pants, I became like a plague to the neighbors who gradually moved further and further away. Since I lost my appetite and gave up eating that I became the regular person on duty to divide the rice into nine portions! I had high fever and could not sleep albeit trying very hard to count numbers in the never ending night.

Sense of Imminent Death

One day I was feeling like my soul was floating in and out of my body. That evening I told Tường that I was going to die. I requested that when he would be free from the camp go inform my family about my death at so and so address. Thanking him for his kindness, I folded my Swiss-made handkerchief neatly, laid my eyeglasses on top of it, put them on the right side of my head, straightened up myself and readied to leave this world for good.

Visitors in POW camp

The next morning, I woke up and found myself still in the shed. By mid-morning, I was informed that I got visitors!

I was exhilarated. I walked briskly towards the gate but at the same time was fully aware that I was like a drunk incapable to keep my path straight.

Anna was there with her Father. They located this unique POW camp for officers in the region through numerous inquiries and difficult travelling conditions. The visit was short, Anna handed me foodstuff and 500 piasters, and promised to return soon.

Dire Prospectus

Anna recounted later that she thought she saw an awful walking corpse: my face was waxy and puffy, eyes dull, clothes tainted with the irksome smell of human waste. My Father-in-law had been a nurse, he predicted that I would not last and kept an eye out for my burial place.

Hospitalization of a POW

A few days later, I was summoned to an above-ground earthen fortification to see the physicians of the Twenty Third Medical Battalion. Fresh aroma of drip coffee drifting in the air and on a shelf there were several cans of sweetened condensed milk; it was Shangri-La in a dungeon! These MDs

were allowed to go out to the market and purchased for the other POWs soy sauce or fermented bean curd.
The doctors told me that I was recommended to go to the local hospital!

A Rip-Off
Since I had no belongings besides my canteen, I went back to the shed to bid farewell to my acquaintances and fetched a motorbike taxi at the gate. The driver asked for 500 piasters. The hospital turned out to be less than a kilometer away; I handed over all my money.

A Vacant Ward
The streets were deserted so was the hospital, whether it was the Phú Bổn Sector Hospital where we had spent one night I did not know. There were a couple clerks in the office and I was led to a ward. The ward linked directly to a kitchen with two big woks; presumably it was part of the kitchen originally and just converted to a patient ward. There were twenty empty bunk beds in two rows, without any bedding or furniture, probably gathered together after the lootings. One patient took up a bed at the end next to the kitchen wall. I was tired and lay down on the middle one.

Speedy Diagnosis
In no time, a man in civilian clothes came, followed by a teenage girl whom was introduced as a nurse trainee. The man told the girl to take my pulse while he checked on me. He told me that what I got was simply malaria. Malaria? I yelled silently within: No way! I never experienced even one bit of shivering the whole time, and now you told me it was malaria? The man said that this was something very common among his comrades; all I had to do was to clinch my teeth and overcome it. He gave me a couple fifty-milligram vitamin C tablets.

Wonder of wonders, after those two just disappeared, Anna rushed in. She came to the POW camp and was so happy to find out that I had been sent to the hospital. She brought along some eggs. She fetched some warm water to wipe me clean.

I had to go to the restroom and the squatting toilets were covered with maggots from wall to wall, so I relieved myself on the cement patch in front of the outhouses. My indecent but reluctant act was caught by that man and he demanded Anna to clean up or else. Anna told me long afterwards that there was nothing available to do the job but using her hands to wipe the spot clean. The repugnant odor stayed on her hands until she washed them over and over with soap. O how she had suffered for me!

Anna stayed for the night and had to leave the next morning, she promised to come back as soon as possible. Some days later, she told me I tried to choke her during the night. It was my first episode of dream walking. Was I trying to kill someone in order to escape, or act out a scene of the action movies, or the delirium had the better of me?

For the patients, the daily meals were rice and water spinach stir fried with beef. The meat was so stringy I gave it to the neighboring malaria patient whom was nursed by his preteen daughter. I went to the big wok trying to boil an egg there, but the water was not hot and the raw egg tasted not that good. I was not sleeping well, in and out of fever I dreamt of many geometric shapes moving around and especially a triangle always poked sharply at my butt, where the daily bleeding was, and woke me up in pain.

The Fall of Saigon

One early morning, I was roused from my stupor by the blasts from the loudspeaker which I did not even know was there on the wall. The announcement put me on rapt attention. It was announcing that yesterday, April 30, they had Saigon

Prisoner of War and "Reeducation"

and the entire South Vietnam liberated; the city of Saigon had been renamed City of Hồ Chí Minh. Military music and songs of victory filled the air.

LIBERATED! I could not believe my ears and was crestfallen. My final hope had been dashed to pieces; I had been hoping that Saigon would be able to hold out and then POWs would be exchanged and go home just as what happened in 1973. Now the whole country had been taken over, how might I live on?

The next day, there were chains of explosions at some distance away. A window pane in the ward shattered and fell on the ground by the shock waves. No one in the ward was trying to move. I walked to the outhouse slowly as usual and suddenly my legs were shaking uncontrollably as by electrical shocks, I embraced the pillar in the middle of the room until the tremor subsided.

In the afternoon, I was informed that I was discharged for my health had improved. I was led to the office and a worker handed me a piece of paper torn from a three by five notebook, on which were written: "Respectfully we repatriate Lt. Quốc to your camp. Signed and dated …" I put the paper into my pocket, the other man spoke up: "This man is not strong enough to leave by himself, why not let him stay till his wife comes." So I was allowed to return to the ward.

A day or two later, Anna came in the morning and she had been told on the way in about my discharge. I asked her to bring me back to the POW camp, because I had no recourse but to follow the order. She thought that I had lost my mind, besides the camp had just moved away. She said: "Let's go home!" So we left the hospital.

Walked Away to Freedom

Off to the market we went. It must be located next to the hospital otherwise I could not make it. We sat down on the tiny wooden stools of a food stand and Anna ordered two bowls of rice soup with duck. That was the most delicious duck soup I ever had. Anna paid for our breakfasts and I found out that they were priced as before. After such a chaotic changeover the currency of the Republic of Vietnam remained in circulation and food prices stayed at the same level; now I understood why our POW physicians could afford drip coffees and sweetened condensed milk.

We stood by the roadside to hitch a ride. After many fast moving military vehicles drove by, finally a truck screeched to stop about 100 feet away from us. I tried to pull myself up and walk fast to the truck but was not able to. I gasped for air every few steps. Anna pulled me along and pushed me up to the truck. We stood behind the driver's cabin and overheard a soldier said to the driver that he should have backed up the truck for the man who was obviously very sick.

While standing on the truck, I felt my pants were getting wet because blood was seeping down. Half an hour or so later Anna requested the driver to let us off. She thanked them for the ride and the truck sped away leaving behind a cloud of dust.

Mother-in-Law's Cabin

It was a small community of less than a hundred houses and shops scattered on either sides of the road. Anna led me into a cabin where her Mother and a few sisters resided. My Mother-in-law welcomed me and Anna tucked me in on a comfortable wooden bed with mosquito net after washing me thoroughly.

Later on, a male nurse came and gave me an injection. The injectable was B-Complex which prescription I gave to Anna when I was in the hospital, supposedly it would help me to regain my appetite. Anna and her brother walked through the open air market in Ban Mê Thuột selling pillaged stuff finally located the medicine displayed on the last poncho at the market's end.

The injectable was in a glass flask with a cork stopper. When the nurse opened the flask, the cork fell in and floated on top of the solution. It was unthinkable that in such a condition I got daily injections retrieved from the flask which was set on top of a cupboard with not even a piece of paper to protect from dusts or insects. I saw that but kept quiet.

After the first injection, my appetite came back in vengence. I finished ten bowls of rice in one sitting. There was no pork for sale because people would not eat pork after witnessing the feral pigs gorged on bloated corpses on Route 7B; therefore we had only squash and salted fish, but I scooped up everything. Since I was so weak, I was in bed most of the time. Gradually my fever came down, diarrhea stopped and no blood in my stools anymore, probably due to the small amount blood remained in me.

Permit from Heaven

One day, many men in fatigues walked on the road. They were ARVN noncoms and soldiers just released from POW camps. A man came in and talked with Anna and her Mom. Somehow the guy got an extra release permit assigned to a man with address in Saigon, since he had no use of it and gave it to Anna. That piece of paper proved to be so needful on my way going back to Saigon, without it I would not be able to register for hotel or purchase a bus ticket.

Since we were in need of money Anna sold my Omega watch to a Chinese woman neighbor who paid 40,000 piasters, and that sum of money came in handy for all the expenses of going home.

Stayed with Father-in-law

After staying with Mom for a couple more days, we departed to go to Anna's Dad. I could not even recall the hitchhike this time.

Walked into Dad's house I saw a large portrait of Uncle Hồ on the altar, it was a compulsory display and joss sticks were burning in front of it. During this period, Dad was doing all the cooking. The daily dish of minnows was so salty I would only take a few bites. Three quarters of the family stayed with my Father-in-law for the older boys had to work on the land to feed the family. It was there I witnessed the first hail storm, kids ran around to collect the marble size hailstones for popsicles. In front of the house were avocado trees; there were many ripened fruits fell from the trees and Anna's sisters mashed them on the ground for fun.

In Dad's house, I kept on sleeping and getting the B-Complex shots from the same unprotected flask. I got serious head lice infestation and went to a neighbor barber to get a free haircut.

My Father-in-law was a man of many talents including tailoring; he sewed me two pairs of shorts for underwear. Dad was a handsome guy and fascinated many ladies. Officially he got a wife and three children in the North. He did not like the arranged marriage and ran away with Anna's Mom to the South in 1954 when Vietnam was split by the Geneva Accords. Anna's grandfather was a high official, the headman of Phủ Lý a suburb of Hà Nội. Dad attended the school for the aristocrats in Hà Nội known as Trường Bưởi, similar to the Eton in Great Britain. Dad had a bitter feud with the Communists because they killed his father. Dad built his own house in Hố Nai of Biên Hòa Province and the bell tower of a church, operated tailor shop and hair salon, etc. He was a jack-of-all-trades but did not stay in any one of them to be prosperous.

Anna had eleven younger brothers and sisters. She had no idea how many half-brothers and half-sisters were out there. Even when there were maids helping out at home, as the big sister Anna always took up the task of running the household. She started to cook for the family at age eight. She witnessed the constant bickering between her parents, in spite of the disharmony a baby came out almost yearly. Anna was so burdened by the role as a Mom substitute because her Mother was always absent from home for business, therefore she was tired of a big family. Her first chore after waking up was to fetch water from the well, wash and hang dry dozens of dirty clothes and urine-drenched blankets. After the half-day school she bathed all the young sisters and dealt with the crybabies. Not only her labors were not appreciated but also blamed for faults not of her own including the anonymous admirers' notes dropped in the house. Anyway, Anna forgave her parents and blamed herself not having sent home more money while they were yet alive.

I was so sick henceforth did not have much interaction with my Father-in-law. Finally, we had to move on; we said goodbye to the family and went to Ban Mê Thuột.

Trip Back Home

On May 22, we boarded a bus to Saigon. By using the unclaimed release permit I was able to stay in the hotel the night before and buy my bus ticket.

Not that far along we came to a bombed-out bridge which was destroyed in the battle in March. Everybody had to leave the bus and waded across the shallow stream except me, for I was considered too frail to do that. (It was around this time that my eldest brother Ju-Hua was coming from the opposite direction to search me out.) The bus crawled slowly on the river bed leaning left and right the whole time. Uneventfully, the bus climbed on the bank and passengers returned to the bus to resume the journey.

The bus driver drove the bus like a sports car when the road was barely wide enough to accommodate two buses. Once when our bus squeezed between an oncoming bus and the row of wooden sheds lining the road, a rearview mirror was shattered and leaving the supporting arm dangling by the side. We were sitting in the second row; fortunately the exploding shards were kept away by the lowered shutters.

Home Alive!

It was Friday, May 23, 1975, after a full day of travel we came to the major bus terminal of Saigon in one piece. Anna fetched a cyclo and we were pedaled home. I had no idea whether my family was still there or had fled abroad or the house was yet standing. Saigon was crowded as before, except the flags of red and blue with yellow stars of the NLF were everywhere. No signs of destruction by the recent warfare were observable. When we were getting closer and closer to home, I tried my best to assure Anna that she would not feel awkward when meeting my folks. The cyclo stopped and Anna paid the fare.

I rang the doorbell. From the second floor balcony Dad saw a total stranger and a Vietnamese woman wearing a traditional conic hat stood at the door, then almost the entire household coming down to see us. No shedding of tears but it was very emotional.

First thing first, I introduced Anna to Mom and Dad, they were quite shocked to see Anna but somewhat relaxed when knowing that because of her I could come home in one piece and noticed her beauty. While we sat down in a circle conversed most of the time in Cantonese, I was apprehending the uneasiness of Anna as a total stranger in our home.

After half an hour or so and the excitement wound down a bit, Anna helped me to take a bath and put on my pajamas. For the trip home, I wore Anna's pants for I had nothing else to wear and they fit me perfectly.

Blood Transfusion

After a quick lunch, my family realized that I needed to be hospitalized. Sitting at the rear of the Lambretta scooter Ju-Xiang drove me to the Grall Hospital, one of the two

French hospitals in Saigon still under foreign control when all other hospitals were in disarray due to looting. Grall Hospital had been known as Đồn Đất Hospital i.e. Hospital on the Earthen Fort.

The female French doctor privately questioned Xiang why I waited for so long before seeking help. A nurse came to get my blood sample. I looked down at the syringe and was astonished to see my blood which was watery and pale red in color, even thinner than the blood found in the thawing ground beef. I was admitted to a private room which my family preferred, and within the hour I got a transfusion. It was amazing that the hospital still had type O blood in the blood bank.

From the patient's chart, my red blood cell count was 1.8 million—about one thirds that of a healthy adult. I weighed a mere forty kilograms, similar to that of Anna, and that was after I ate like a horse for more than two weeks; usually my weight ranged from sixty to sixty five kilos. The doctor prescribed me three doses of three Fansidar pills each, seven days apart. Previously I learned that one dose of Fansidar, a miracle drug for malaria by then, would be sufficient to treat malaria, and she prescribed me three times as much. The lab test confirmed that I got Plasmodium falciparum, the most malicious type of malaria. For my swollen feet, another doctor gave me a strong dose of cortisone, the swelling went away the next day.

Anna came with my parents to see me and then stayed with me most of the time during my hospitalization. She slept in a cot as the customary way for nursing family member. She wanted to go back home for having accomplished her mission to bring me home safely, and was very uncomfortable when she found out that I was Chinese. How could I allow her to do so although she had not been officially accepted by my family but she had been my wife in the truest sense! Besides, the social situation was so unstable that none of us knew what was coming. I begged her to stay.

I stayed in Grall Hospital for ten days. At dusk, a nurse would come with a tray of sleeping pills for the patients to pick and choose. As I had no problem of sleeping anymore so I declined each time. In the ward, a mother grieved about her son who was blinded by tear gas in the student demonstration against the disintegrating South Vietnamese government in the last days of April.

In addition to the hospital regimen, my family brought in nutritious food, especially the broth made from hand-chopped beef to replenish iron for blood. One day, after finishing the beef, I did not want to waste the residual broth still in the bowl so I finished them all. Subsequently I was unable to breathe for a few seconds and nearly die from it. From then on, I learned my lesson not to kill myself from overeating.

To check my hemorrhoids colorectal exam was carried out. I was put in the knee-chest position and a physician inserted a scope of stainless steel tube nearly a meter long after it had been brought up to body temperature in warm water. The doctor saw nothing abnormal in my colon and rectum; he found not even one hemorrhoid. I guessed that all my varicose veins were deflated when all the remaining blood was concentrated in the vital organs.

After the hospital stay I put on ten kilograms. My brother Ju-Xiang told me that I went home because a Public Security cadre raised questions on my identity to the hospital staff; otherwise I would stay in the hospital much longer.

Wedding Rite

A few days later, on an auspicious day according to the Chinese zodiac, Mom led me and Anna to the altar of ancestors for a wedding ceremony. With the customary steamed whole chicken, and cooked vegetables on display. We bowed to the ancestral plaque and offered joss sticks, poured out three cups of rice wine and tea. Mom gave Anna some jewelry; by the witness of heaven and earth and ancestors Anna became part of the family.

Luck or Fate

On many occasions, I was blamed for the failure of the family to flee Vietnam. I wondered if I did manage to return to Saigon, what kind of authority a 2nd Lt. had that could bring the family out by way of the U.S. Embassy or the Port of Saigon? Many generals and high power officials wound up in "reeducation" and whom could they blame for the decision to stay behind instead of leaving Vietnam?

A high school classmate got away through his younger brother in the Navy. My buddy Vương Chiêu successfully escorted his Commodore's thirty plus family members but could not bring along one of his own. My brother Ju-Xiang was on the chaotic scene of the U.S. Embassy but unable to beat the crowd; he got in a helicopter but had to return due to fee-for-service conflict between the pilots and their boss.

Excess Sweating

My health was still much to be desired; my recuperating nervous system induced excessive sweating from head to toe at mealtime, so I had to change my clothes. (It took about two months for the symptom to go away, by then I was already on the subsistence diet in the "reeducation" camp.)

Daily life for us was primarily the same although the atmosphere had become very stressful. The omnipresent loudspeakers blasted propaganda from dawn to dusk on every street corner. The portraits of Hồ Chí Minh, flags of the Provisional Revolutionary Government of South Vietnam and red banners were everywhere. Former government offices became those of the Public Security, People's Soviets and Committees. A confiscated house across from ours became the office of the Patriotic Student Union.

Streets Without Joy

The happy faces I could see were of the Communist cadres and soldiers, or the "patriotic" components—for them a new term was coined "The Thirty" or "April Thirtieth", the opportunists of the time. The faces of the people looked haggardly. Businesses, banks, factories, and schools were shut, people had no work; what happened to those living from hand to mouth was hard to imagine. The currency of the former South was kept in circulation that was not only unheard of but also helped to prevent a total collapse of social order. There were some price increases but not across the board, many commodities were not available openly anymore.

In contrast with the situation in Cambodia when the Khmer Rouge took over that country, South Vietnam's fate was not as bad, the military and government personnel, and the intelligentsia in the South had not been summarily eradicated in the changeover.

A friend of Dad emerged as a Chinese Communist supporter; hoping that Anna and I might obtain assistance to reenter the household registry, we went to see him. He was still friendly to us, but apparently could not be of any help. The Chinese Communist sympathizers participated in the struggle against the Government of Vietnam for decades, especially among the textile factory workers and journalists, yet soon after the fall of the South they were not much better than those who had nothing to with the Communist, it was obvious that the Vietnamese Communists schemed to spin out of the sphere of influence of China and align with the U.S.S.R. instead.

"Reeducation" Decrees

In early June, an order was announced to all the ARVN soldiers, noncoms (including CWOs), police and common government workers of the Republic of Vietnam report for a three-day "reeducation." In Saigon, these people were to bring their own lunches reporting to the neighborhood schools in the morning and return home in the evening.

Accordingly, my eldest brother Ju-Hua attended the "reeducation" course, after three days he got a stenciled certificate of citizenship. Wow, the Provisional Revolutionary Government or the "Revolution" as they called themselves kept its word and granted amnesty to the "Counterfeit Regime" and the "Counterfiet Military"! On June 16, former senior government officials, officers from the rank of Major and up should report for a month-long "reeducation." They were to bring clothing, rice or meal money sufficient for thirty days. Obviously this order was quite welcomed since the "Revolution" did keep their promise in the "reeducation" of the soldiers. After all, blood was thicker than water, was not this the time to forget the painful past and join hands to build a new Vietnam?

Right after the senior personnel had gone, another decree came: junior officers must report to ten-day "reeducation": Captains on June 23rd and 24th, First Lieutenants 25th, 26th, and Second Lieutenants 27th, 28th.

Anna pleaded me not to go. For me, it was not that easy to hide away from all the watchful eyes of the new rulers and the opportunistic informants. Besides, I naively presumed that the political development in South Vietnam was monitored by the entire world; therefore the government would keep its word as it had just done to the soldiers.

Preparation for "Reeducation"

Preparing for my ten-day "educational trip", off we went to the Central Market of Saigon. None of the hats could fit my head, so I settled for an extremely tight wide-brim nylon hat. Shoes were for the bourgeois class, I bought a pair of plastic sandals.

For the excessive sweating, I would stay away from taking cold water bath but trash my smelly clothes after every three days. I squeezed into an old travel bag three changes of well-worn long-sleeved shirts and dress pants, an old mosquito net with many patches, a nylon tablecloth for bed sheet, an old blanket, a plastic bottle, washcloth and toiletries.

I had contacted my friends Lương Tô and Lư Tô to report as a group in the Fifth District. At the last minute they changed their plans and went to their home district instead. I got to go alone.

Brother Ju-Xiang drove me to the designated high school on the scooter on Thursday afternoon, June 24— the deadline for First Lieutenants. The school was on Hồng Bàng Street with only a few soldiers guarding the gate. I signed in at a table and was directed to a large empty warehouse, assigned to a unit of ten guys, among them Hồ Kim whom I recognized at once a Cantonese.

The atmosphere was like a toned-down reunion; I bumped into two OCS classmates from the Forty Third Company: Hồ văn Anh and Khúc Ngọc Bảo, both were VNAF Military Police. They got all the advantages to flee the country at the last days yet chose to stay.

Around the warehouse, no NVA cadres or soldiers were in sight, but we behaved ourselves. After finishing our own dinners, we slept on the floor in the assigned area. I imagined that we would stay in the school and have our ten-day lessons.

After midnight, there came the order to move. Unit by unit we climbed into the military trucks with canvas canopy. After a long wait, the column rolled.

Camp Trảng Lớn

By dawn, we arrived at Trảng Lớn, an ARVN base in Tây Ninh Province near the Cambodian border. We got off the trucks and went to designated quarters.

My unit of ten got a bunker built with sand-filled ammunition crates. There was a big hole in the center of the roof, probably blasted through by a mortar shell not that long ago, and the floor was plain dirt. We were the first group arrived, without much discussion, we hunted around and moved enough pallets for our quarters. I was too weak to help in carrying anything weighty, looking around and found on a windowsill six or seven canteen cups; I kept one for myself and passed on the rest to the others. I took up my position under the gaping hole because all better spots have been grabbed, since the ground beneath me had been dug up by the explosion so I got a wider berth.

We ten people belonged to a basic unit called an "A", higher up was a "B" which always consisted of twenty guys, and a "C" varied from a handful to a dozen of "B"s.

We were assigned a mail code "Hòm Thư (Mail Box) 7590". In the vocabulary of the Northerner hòm meant box; in the South, the word had an exclusive meaning: coffin. For us the word was amusing and uncomfortable at the same time, because it linked to death. In my mind, the number 7590 also implied that we might have to stay in the camp from 1975 to 1990; for some it turned out to be correct.

Trần Viết Hùng was appointed our "A" leader. A guy from the neighboring A was designated as head of the B who brought back instructions after attending meetings with the cadres. Those cadres were called quản-giáo or discipliners, obviously we were prisoners.

Trảng Lớn was a huge base; we found many brand-new machine-gun ammunition boxes in two different sizes that we could use as pots, water or food containers. I kept two ammo boxes until the day I left camp in 1978.

The other nine First Lieutenants were: Hồ Kim from the Rangers, he was in the commodity service called Quân Tiếp Vụ which distributed rice, cooking oil, canned goods, cigarettes etc. to the troops and their dependents. Somehow Kim and I remained together in the same A for nearly three years, which was extremely rare because we were broken up frequently to form new units. Nguyễn Hưng Đạo, Phan Thành

Trung, and Nguyễn văn Hoàng were in the Navy; Nguyễn Hữu Khai, Huey UH-1B helicopter pilot; Nguyễn văn Nam, VNAF English instructor; Cao văn Minh, AC-119 gunship pilot; Trần Viết Hùng, Sub-sector Chief; and Nguyễn văn Ân, a high school teacher who was short but had long stories about his "adventures" in the Special Forces, such as shooting daggers from his forearm by a strapped-on mechanism. Most teachers were discharged from the ARVN after finishing the OCS, but they were still on the Reserve Officer roster.

No order had been given to collect our meal money or rice. From the first day, we got two bowls of cooked rice at noon and late afternoon, the same ration I got in the POW camps. One guy brought along some brown rice, so Trung and Đạo went around and found a shovel to break up some creosote poles to cook the rice in an ammo box. The smoke from the firewood was thick, black and acrid but nobody paid attention to the toxic fumes, all we cared about was the stomach. On one occasion, our food was supplemented by boiled banana flower heart which was wrenched from a banana bush by our Navy guys. Pretty soon, a reminder came that anyone caught stealing "the People's properties" would be disciplined.

One day there was a commotion outside. One guy of the adjoining "A" was scalded by the exploding hot water from an ammo box: when he tried to open the box which was clasped tightly by the rubber-lined lid, the hot water and vapor under high pressure released like a bomb. Our buddy got half of his body in second degree burn. The teammates spread toothpaste all over him; from this we got a valuable lesson in using the ammo boxes.

Trăng Lớn was an U.S. Army base and there were runways, chopper landing pads, and fortifications built from perforated steel planking, from which we salvaged some rectangular connector pins to use as hammers. From the very first day on, harvesting and storing up things that might be useful became a routine.

Days dragged on but no lessons, not even political propaganda whatsoever had been given. Someone raised the question to the quản-giáo and was told to be patient because we were just settling down and we would be let go when were good through "reeducation". What was the definition of "good", then? The answer was like a clap of thunder, even though we heard it indirectly: "Good is when we say you are good!"

We naïvely trusted the order of ten-day "reeducation", they trapped the senior officers first and then the junior ones. Leaders of the former Republic of Vietnam had been put away for good. Besides, the standard of good by the NVA that years later got us released was not up to par to that of the Public Security or of the local governments.

One day, an entire A nearby was disciplinarily confined to a ship container for a week because one guy disappeared by hiding in a delivery truck. That was the first prison break that I knew.

Later on, some had been caught climbing the barbed wire fence and were shot or executed later; and a few got away from the camp were caught en route to their homes.

We were able to roam freely after dinner and I encountered some Chinese friends, among them Hoàng Minh Tân a classmate from the Military Medicine School. Tân informed me that a soldier could buy us things and even deliver mails for us Chinese. So I sent home a note and got response a week later with some money and a little bit of food. The soldier was amazed at the affluence of our homes and he was rewarded for his courier service.

In the center of our bunker was a square column, we used a charred chip to mark our stay there. On day forty two, August 7, we got order to move.

A Touching Scene

Our moving trucks were not covered with tarpaulins, when we came to the edge of Tây Ninh City, the convoy stopped for a brief moment next to a roadside market. Suddenly some men and women threw baguettes and glutinous rice cakes into our trucks.

Probably the leader sensed something wrong, therefore the convoy began to roll, but still a few people ran after us to hand out more food. All of us were deeply moved by the acts of compassion, we waved to them in silence until we saw them no more. We shared the fresh bread without a word but just glanced at each other. Only three months after the fall of the South, these people recognized the differences between the two regimes and were sympathetic to those they knew were ARVN officers in bonds.

Camp Long-Khánh

We were trucked to Long-Khánh where the last big battle was fought. A reinforced Eighteenth Division tied down a NVA Corps for two weeks before they could approach Saigon. The commanding general of the division Lê Minh Đảo was kept in the North for seventeen years and eventually came to the States. The place we came was of the Eighteenth Medical Battalion, and medicines were found in the ruins by some. There I bumped into dentist Hoàng of our II Corps Dispensary, pharmacist Trị of the 721 Medical Supply Depot in Pleiku, and physician Trần văn Nhậm of the Phú Phong Sectoral Dispensary in Bình Định Province.

After a short while, we got our first ration of tobacco and cane sugar squares, each one got two ounces of tobacco and four squares of sugar. For the nonsmokers, we traded the tobacco for two squares of sugar. The smokers used all kinds of papers available to roll up the tobacco, and pipes were improvised from the aluminum tubes of discharged flares. Addiction was nearly impossible to stay away, one guy roasted portion of his rice into imitation coffee.

Hundreds of us were put in one huge warehouse. When evening came, long cords were stretched across the place for people to latch on their mosquito nets. At night it was in near total darkness and we slept in very tight quarters. It posed a big problem for me. I lied in the middle of the crowd and every night I had to release myself at least once due to my yet weak bladder control. Carefully, I fumbled in the dark crawling on all fours over people's feet and heads, maneuvered between the mosquito nets without crushing anybody or pulling the nets down or tearing them apart. Fortunately, after a week or so, the big group split into Cs and assigned to newly prepared quarters.

A barbed wire partition fence was set up making it very hard to communicate from either side.

Housing Arrangement

We moved to the row houses previously housed the families of the Medical Battalion. Like most ARVN housings they were built by cement blocks with galvanized corrugated tin roofs. Each A fit snugly into one house which had lain neatly with plywood probably taken down from the ceilings. The plywood extended about six feet from the wall leaving room for a walkway from the front to the back; the rear was an open area with a covered outhouse. I had no idea how long these row houses been vacant but the open area was covered with weeds and the drain hole of the toilet was filled with pebbles and rocks. One guy cleaned out the rocks and dirt from the toilet and it worked fine for us during our stay there.

At once, we spied around and brought back empty cannon powder canisters, some were six feet tall, some three, as water containers.

A Suicide

Within a fortnight, news spread across the camp: a pharmacist on the other side of the partition hanged himself.

Living Conditions

Tree branches and trunks cut roughly to a yard in length were trucked in and rationed to each "A" to split up as firewood for the common kitchen.

We found a couple short barbed wire posts, flattened and sharpened them into two broadsword-like woodchoppers. By pounding the smaller limbs on the choppers we split the big trunks. The tools we had were so primitive; hitting the woodchopper with brute force usually broke up several smaller branches before we could split a big one. Afterwards we stacked up the firewood to dry under the sun. Nothing would be wasted; we swept up all the splinters and leaves for fuel.

Necessity brought out ingenuity: well covers were transformed into buckets, guitars made from the extra plywood, guitar strings from phone wires, cords out of nylon sandbags, shorts out of cloth sandbags, utensils and footwear from salvaged materials.

When patches appeared on our worn-out clothing, we caricatured ourselves the Beggar Gang as in the well-known Kim-Dung novels. Medical doctors used the aluminum cans of Guigoz milk powder for cooking, we called them "Doctor Can Guigoz" resembling the doctor in the film "Doctor Zhivago"—a hard life under Communist rule that we were going through.

These trapped people were pillars of the society in the South: professors, teachers, physicians, pharmacists, dentists, engineers, lawyers, agricultural specialists, pilots, captains, and technicians. Here we were wasting away our lives for crimes against the "People."

There was no works for us and we had so much free time on hand, therefore different associations and classes were formed. Some gave physiology/health classes, some taught algebra and calculus, some even organized body-building sessions on the subsistence diet with barbells made from cement blocks and metal pipes. Nobody dared to form literary or language classes.

Somebody salvaged the canopy support frames from a GMC truck and did not know what to do with those molded plywood until the idea of making a mahjong set came up. One guy used an improvised saw to cut the wood into mahjong pieces and then rubbed them against the wall or the curb to make them uniform as best as they could. Out of the handful of Chinese in the C the mahjong group solicited my help to put the Chinese characters on the game pieces. I used black and red ball point pens to imprint the Chinese characters. I stopped to play the mahjong after it changed from pastime to gambling; people used sugar, cigarette or even money as wagers.

One day a roommate told me that I was seen crawled out of the mosquito net, sat on the edge of the plywood sheet and sanding an unseen mahjong piece in my hand on the wall. I knew now why I tried to choke Anna at the Phú Bổn Hospital. I had no idea whether I still sleepwalk today.

In Long-Khánh, I was shown the game of Scrabble. The adjoining A had several English instructors, and Vũ Hoàng Chương was one with the VNAF. Chương made the Scrabble pieces from cardboard and the game board from brown paper. He used to play with his friends for money, a dollar for a point. I was the one that played with him most frequently, because the other instructors including Nam in my A were neither good nor interested in it. Even with Chương's experience he was beaten on the game more and more by me. The best word I had was SNOW which made five words. We had no dictionary and Chương was easygoing in agreeing with me a few strange words that I put down.

On one occasion I got a page from the U.S. News and World Report out of a paper bag, I went through it many times and hid it in my travel bag.

English instructor Lý Tô Hán, a Cantonese, became newsworthy among our B for a while. In the evening we had the luxury of a couple hours of electricity; one evening Hán cried fire when he saw sparks on the power lines and they turned out to be fireflies.

In the evening, I liked to stroll in the courtyard with a C-47 pilot Đoàn Tử Bằng and chatted softly in English. Bằng and Nguyễn Đông Sơn, a Regional Force Company Commander, were interested in learning conversational Cantonese; so I taught them, separately. They already had rudimentary knowledge of Cantonese and picked it up very fast and were able to carry on basic conversation with me. Unfortunately, they both died in a horrendous ammunition dump explosion later on.

Political Lessons

Two months or so after we settled down in the row houses we were readying for lessons. Money was collected for notebooks and ballpoint pens; each made a stool to sit in the "auditorium"—the warehouse that we had slept in previously. We were kind of excited that the "process" had finally begun.

It was the first time I saw a political cadre with his insignias of Captain on the shoulder boards. The NVA had more ranks than we did; they followed the Soviet system that added an extra rank in each echelon. They had Capt. on top of Upper Lt., Col. atop Upper-Col., and Gen. above the four-star Upper Gen. For the Allies, stars were reserved for the General Officers but NVA from Private to General all studded with them.

In the indoctrination sessions which always started out with patriotic songs and praises to Uncle Hồ. We knew many of the tunes well from the loudspeakers hitting our eardrums day in and day out.

Secretive exchanges from someone who had lived under Communist rule gave me deep thought after I became a Christian: the atheistic Communist system fashioned after the Church with the Party playing god. After the Tiananmen massacre of June 4, 1989, many Chinese students in the States turned to Christ. They were astonished at first when attending Bible study; it was so similar to what they had gone through in studying the Small Red Book of Mao Ze-Dong, interspersed with songs and self-critique.

During the political session quản-giáo strolled up and down the hall and we all seemingly paying attention to the lecture. It was hard to hold our peace when the propaganda were so absurd. We mimicked a cadre who pronounced Iran as "one ran" and Iraq "one raq."

After a two-hour session we returned to the row houses for discussions and self-critique. We always spoke loud and clear when a quản-giáo was nearby; otherwise we just looked around till the gong sounded the end of a session.

The indoctrination consisted of eight lessons and the cycle repeated through the years. Out of the eight lessons I could only recall the first two. Lesson one: The American Empire is the Enemy Number One of all the peoples of the world. Lesson two: Vietnam is the navel of the universe, the conscience of mankind.

All the people from the North were identical in their way of propagandizing through repetitive indoctrination.

We were required to write confession after we "realized" our crimes against the People and the Party in serving the Counterfeit Regime, the Counterfeit Army, and as lackeys to the American Imperialists.

We were encouraged to report if we knew of people or whereabouts that had hidden weapons or treasures, in turn we would go home sooner.

They claimed to be patriotic and swore to uproot all colonial influences, but in daily language still retained French words that could readily be replaced, such as frein for brake, or un deux for one-two in marching.

Twice a day at mealtime, an "orderly" from each A would go to the common kitchen to pick up the group's rations. With aluminum basins filled with rice set on top of the stove beside the big wok, by rotation, the orderly would pick the seemingly bigger basin. On returning, he would divide the rice into ten portions and waited for the last share after the other nine made their choice. So no matter it was in the common kitchen or in our living quarters every one learned to be very fair in dividing the portions.

We heard that the rice we ate had been stored underground in rubber plantations for years, therefore some of us developed a benign form of vitamin B1 deficiency, like Vũ Hoàng Chương "the Scrabble master" would suddenly collapse while walking. The recommendation was that those patients should take advantage of the morning sun and were given some rice soup skimmed from the big wok when rice was being cooked. Obviously, vitamin B1 came from old rice and from sunlight.

Grand Theft Fishes

Each A would take turn to cook rice for the C. One day, we were on duty and it was the only time we got fish; it happened to be also a day for political lesson, so everybody stayed inside except the cooks on duty. One among us suggested that it was an opportunity to take advantage of and no one objected to that great idea! Pretending to be busy preparing the fish and rice, we carried the ammo boxes filled with raw fish back to our house. On that day, everyone in the C got about five ounces of fish but the ten of us had enough for an entire week.

We were always on the lookout to gather extra food. By the recommendation from Ân the tall-story guy, some of us tried to cook rose moss with which the farmers sometimes used to feed their pigs and the resulting soup tasted as bland as ... water.

Scavenging

On a couple occasions, a food truck parked next to our houses after unloading vegetables and rock salts; we scraped off from the flatbed of the truck to collect that tiny bit of spilled watery salts. We dissolved the muck in water, cleaned out the dirt and boiled the brine into table salt. We salvaged all the hardy green coverings of cabbage and the leafy tops of turnip to make pickles.

Fried Crickets

One day I saw an empty can got thrown away from the guards' kitchen and it rolled to the barbed wire fence. After making sure no one was around I used a bamboo stick to pick up the can through a fence opening; I maneuvered the stick into the triangular opening punctured on the top of the can, lifting it up so I could grab it.

Initially I needed the can as a container but I noticed that there was oil clinging to the can; by flipping up the can and I got a spoonful of leftover oil. With oil in place, Minh the AC-119 pilot went out to the earthen mounds to dig up the big crickets which had always been a delicacy in the South. Then Minh, Hồ Kim, and I had crispy fried crickets for meals. I had gotten about five oil cans that way and we ate many fried crickets.

The reason I bothered to salvage the cans because I had brought along a C-ration can opener; I also had a nail clipper, these tools turned out to be very useful for many.

The only living things that could crawl around alive in our living quarters were the huge black snails called ghost snails. I presumed that the snails were either poisonous or malodorous; otherwise nobody would ignore such a bountiful supply of protein.

Every morning, for roll call our C of 200 or so listless people gathered in the courtyard in loose formation, the C leader took a count from the A's then turned about-face to report to the quản-giáo standing high up on the veranda. Old habit died hard, one day our C leader turned around to report and unconsciously raising his hand to salute the quản-giáo, at that split second he realized what he had done, swiftly he dropped his hand and turned back. None of us dare to laugh until the quản-giáo laughed out first.

We did not "labor" in Long-Khánh except once we were mobilized to go out of the camp to gather broken concrete blocks and bricks to spread them on a section of the road. By rumor the road was readied for family visit!

One day, several people were called to gather their belongings and move away: they were Police or Sub-sector Chiefs reassigned to the custody of the Interior Ministry while we remained under the Military Control Committee of Hồ Chí Minh City. So from our B Trần Viết Hùng and a gray-haired guy went away. Those "vile elements" had been accused of maltreating and torturing the Commies and their sympathizers, but who knew if these folks were not taken out of this place, some among them might have suffered a horrible death later on?

After the departure of Hùng, our A stayed nine in count until the unexpected uprooting of the camp.

Sometime in November, we were allowed to write letter home. Fully aware that our mails would be censored by the camp cadres and the Public Security at home, so I said all things were fine and the government was good in treating us. We were allowed to receive a gift package of one kilogram from home, no staples were allowed for that could be used for escape. Some among us did not even receive a gift pack due to all sorts of reasons.

Picture from Home

In the letter from home came along with the package was the picture of a month-old baby girl lying in a lounge chair taken in a portrait studio. I proudly showed the picture around and no one had problems in recognizing her likeness to me.

Even with the subsistence diet of stale rice, my body improved gradually and I could do better than some others like Hồ Kim. I was the second strongest guy in our A, after Minh, to carry the water buckets, one in each arm, to bring water from a well fifty yards away without stopping. The buckets were tinkered from galvanized well covers therefore very heavy. The more convenient way to get water was to channel rainwater from the gutters to the howitzer tubes in the back or the fuel drum in the front.

In order to get more water, some deepened the existing wells and others planned to dig a new one. It was a good test of the feng shui some firmly believed in to locate a good spot. One guy identified an underground spring using a "home-made" compass from twigs. After sinking to a depth of about eight meters the well was blocked by granite. Though the excavators tried hard to circumvent the blockage but it was impossible to squeeze through the narrow passage between the dirt wall and the sharp rock, therefore the project was given up.

The first Christmas silently went by, then the New Year of 1976.

Failed Escape

One evening we were hurriedly ordered to gather in the courtyard, and three guys were paraded before us. Four men escaped from our camp and were caught by the militia. During the night, one man used a pottery shard to slit his own wrist but failed because the tool was blunt, so he begged the others to finish him off, and one did.

After a month of confinement two guys returned to their own groups but the "executioner" was staying alone in a ship container situated in the wide open space between the outer perimeter and the inner barbed wire fence backing our row houses. Occasionally, I saw him sitting in front of the connex tinkering with sheet metals or mending clothes.

In my teenage years, we used to read a Chinese magazine titled "World of Today" published by the now defunct U.S. News Agency and printed in Hong Kong. Besides the news on the West were reports on the Communist world. Many of the then incredible reports about the Iron Curtains in that publication turned out to be true. For example, a soldier went back North on furlough, his hen laid one egg in the morning and another one at night!

A young guy in the neighboring A got an early release, but with a very grim prospect. The 2nd Lt. was in the infantry got run over by an M113 Armored Personnel Carrier; he suffered difficulty in urination due to the traumatized pelvis therefore was discharged from the ARVN, but he still had to report to "reeducation." On a couple occasions he was moaning and groaning with pain and a doctor used a recycled plastic syringe to relieve his bloating bladder. We could only wish him luck, inside or outside the camp, access to medical care was very limited.

Two Films

During this time we had been shown movies. A silver screen was erected for the occasions, and we were reminded to bring our stools. One film was produced by an Eastern Bloc country; it was in color and voiced over in Vietnamese. We laughed when hearing the title of the movie: "The Kingdom of Deception." It was so true that we all had been deceived by such a kingdom. I had no memory of the plot of the movie; it was in medieval settings and was done quite well in my opinion.

On the other occasion, the documentary was a very memorable one. It was a black-and-white propaganda film titled "Farewell, Uninvited Guests." It recorded from the capture of downed U.S. pilots, the life of POWs in the Hanoi Hilton—Hỏa Lò Prison up to their release on February 12, 1973. The atmosphere was heavy, for we were not only watching what our allies had gone through but also in much worse conditions than ours. When they were first captured, they were bound and paraded under gunpoint, greeted by rocks, cursing, and spitting. In prisoner garbs they were interviewed in press conferences. They opened packages sent through the Red Cross, and read mails from home. When the U.S. POWs were intently picking out the bigger rice portions, we burst into laughter. The most touching scene was the release ceremony when the POWs walked towards the C-141 Starlifter on the tarmac of Gia Lâm Airport; some were limping, some on clutches or on stretchers. When passing by the Stars and Stripes everyone saluted the flag and the welcoming General beneath it. For us, our flag was no more and no delegation would receive us home.

Lessons for Life

In the indoctrination classes I learned several things: the Party and the People were exceedingly lenient, all the crimes committed by us under the "Counterfeit Regime" and "Counterfeit Military" had been forgiven; but, our past would be on file for three generations: our grandchildren would be barred from higher education and employment opportunities. Anyone was not with "The People" was against "The People", even those civilians who did not stand with them in the "Revolution against the aggressors" were also branded "Counterfeit Citizens."

We were taught also that in order for the "Revolution" to win, the Party would use all means to attain its goal. When the "anti-revolutionary" was strong, they would use the "two steps forward and one step backward" tactics diplomatically inching up to their advantage; once they were in a superior position then negotiation was no more necessary. After they had won over the support of the "peace-loving peoples" of the world they had no need to hide behind the banner of Labor Party but reverted to its original name Communist Party of Vietnam. They emphasized the saying of Lenin that he would use the ropes sold him by the capitalists to hang them.

Times flew and it was late April and we were in another cycle of indoctrination class to bring in the first anniversary of April 30.

Deadly Explosion

April 29, 1976. Lunch was over and we sat in a circle on our plywood beds pretending to discuss the morning lesson "The Great Victory of Spring." Suddenly, there were sounds of firecrackers and I wondered why people could not wait till tomorrow to ignite their fireworks. In no time, the sounds became louder and denser. We turned our heads to the courtyard and saw with horror bullets and stuffs fell to the ground, and big explosions followed.

We arose and dispersed to all directions. Hồ Kim and I went to the rear, sat down with our backs leaning on the wall and considered what to do next. We could not go any further from our rear exit because it had been blocked by barbed wires. Then a big explosion loosened some bricks from the eaves, one hit Kim on the head and one my left shoulder. The strong gust from the explosion pushed open the barbed wire mesh and I rushed out through that opening.

The best way to minimize the danger was to widen the distance away from the ammo dump which we never knew. I ran by the "executioner's connex" and it was empty, swiftly I went inside. I sat down and congratulated myself for finding a bomb shelter protected by thick iron walls on all sides. From nowhere, a strange sensation came and urged me to leave, without hesitation I got up and went outside. Sat down with my back reclining to the shipping container and faced east opposite to the direction from whence the explosions came, I found a fuel drum lid and held it above my head to guard from things falling down from above.

Soon after I went outside three guys ran into the connex; I heard their laughters and exciting exchanges. They must be very happy for finding such a secure place from harm's way. After a minute or so, there was a loud explosion on the west side of the connex and I heard a loud cry: "He's dead, he's dead!" Two men ran off. Immediately, I too ran away from the connex toward the east, the further away from the ammunition dump the better. Some other guys like me were stopped short of the perimeter fence because the guards would shoot anyone getting near.

If this was not a life-threatening event it was surely a wonderful firework display. Roaring rockets twirled around with colorful smoke trails, countless puffs of white and black smokes floating in the sky after detonating on various altitudes.

I crouched behind a tree and happened to look to the far right seeing a large piece of shiny metal falling from the sky; it fell on a guy who was hiding behind a rusted WWII Japanese tank like a big cleaver. Too frightened to watch I shut my eyes.

Clean-Up

It was before sunset that the explosions died out. We were ordered to carry the wounded to the camp's dispensary. I remembered seeing distilled water being produced by heating a flask with an alcohol burner. Inside a mosquito net, a corpse lying on his side exposing a buttock with cutting marks like a checkerboard; he might have died from the probing cuts rather than from shrapnel wounds.

We trudged back to our sleeping quarters with care for sharp metal pieces were all over. I got a glimpse of the waxy corpse reclining at the door of the connex; one leg was folded at the shin and pointed upwards. If not due to the unintelligible urging to go out, that corpse might be me!

Ammo Disposal & Ten Coffins
Next day, the historical April 30 did not come with any celebration. We were to get rid of the unexploded ordnances. A well in the back of our row houses was designated as the disposal pit for all the intact ammo found. Under the guidance of one who was with the Ordnance Command we picked up the bullets, grenades and shells. Our buddy cautioned us to pay extra care to the M-79 grenades, with the same way they were lying on the ground tried not to twitch one bit of their orientation to minimize the chance of detonation.

Coffins were delivered to the camp, and all the coffins in Long-Khánh were sold. I had no idea of the casualties of civilians or that of our own in the surrounding camps. Just in our C of about 500-600 souls, ten perished—including my Cantonese students Bằng and Sơn, and a handsome guy in the Special Forces.

The atheistic Communists supposedly had nothing to do with the opiate of the masses, but they provided candles and joss sticks for us to offer to the decedents. Our deaths were placed in a row across from the connex; I did not go to view them, it was too much for me!

We noticed a corner of our roof in the front was shagging, using a roughly built ladder I climbed up and saw a howitzer shell lying in the gutter.

An Unforgettable Image
Standing on the ladder looking west to the origin of the explosions, I saw a picture not painted by human hands. On the backdrop of a bombed-out ruin, the one thing remained

standing against the flattened horizon under a clear blue morning sky was the A-frame of a bell tower, a bell was still hanging under the horizontal beam and a cross perching on the apex. I was awestruck and climbed down the ladder slowly.

Until I became a Christian then I understood that in this unique occasion, the inerasable image of a cross standing aloof in the ruin of destruction revealed the significance of the cross to me was by divine design.

Hồ Kim suffered a small crack on the skull by the falling brick; another one hit my left shoulder blade and left a permanent scar. My wound got infected and I bumped into Trị the pharmacist from Pleiku on the other side of the partition; through the barbed wire fence he gave me eight capsules of antibiotic and the wound was healed.

The nine of us ran to different directions during the explosion, but many others just hid in their row houses. Although these dwellings were built with cement blocks but they withstood the violent forces. Our common kitchen suffered a roof collapse and the big wok got a big chunk cut away, so we got rice to cook for ourselves.

Probably due to the nearness of Long-Khánh to Saigon and the extraordinary destructive power of the explosion, the news could not be suppressed, we were told to write home at once. Hoàng from the Navy told his family all the details of the explosion that he knew of, for he bet that neither the cadres nor the Public Security would have time to censor all the letters. I just wrote a few lines that I was safe and sound.

At the same time, the A leaders were to compile a listing so as to replenish our clothing got destroyed in the catastrophe. I did not lose any clothing but I pushed my luck and reported that I had lost three sets. On the very next day I got three sets of brand-new ARVN fatigues, apparently we had left a whole lot behind in the depots. I asked a guy who worked in the Quartermasters' sewing factory to help make a bag; he used some charred wood sketched out an outline of a travel bag with shoulder strap on a shirt, by a knife he cut out all the component pieces in no time. In the same day, I sewed up the bag; the shirt pockets became side pockets with buttoned flaps.

Camp Long-Giao

After a week or so we got order to move. We moved to the nearby military base of Long-Giao which was also a former U.S. base with the typical wooden barracks but the grounds previously covered by crushed stones had mostly gone. Saturated with spring rain, muds were all over the place, a thick layer of mud glued to our footwear.

In the camp, there was only one well about fifteen meters deep and we had to lengthen the ropes of our water buckets to fetch water. With so many of us, we needed more water and some volunteered to deepen the well. Without mechanical ventilation or ladder it was quite a hazardous undertaking; our exhausted diggers came up like mud men. Their hard work availed us with more water.

There were plenty of aloe plants around the camp and we found on the underside of those leaves names with ranks and dates; it turned out that many senior officers had been kept there before shipped to the north.

Jungle of Katum

Again we moved, as usual at nighttime in those made-in-China trucks. After several hours, we heard the faint sounds of gong and the column slowed down when it hit the dirt road. Someone opened a flap of the tarpaulin and we saw some guys working by the roadside; one of us put two fingers on his collar and the response was one, they were Second Lieutenants.

We were in Katum near the border of Cambodia, a vast jungle. The trucks dropped us off in a small opening. After the quản-giáo from Long-Giao handed us over to the local ones, they departed. Our A had been scattered, only Hồ Kim and I were staying together. A handful of us were led to another spot. A guy wearing a blue Playboy cap with half of the visor torn from the seam came to greet us; I felt amused if the quản-giáo knew what that bunny stood for. The man introduced himself as Nguyễn văn Bê, our B leader. He led us to a small thatched hut.

The hut was for our A which had several vacancies because some had moved to a "model" camp near a "New Economic Zone". The hut and the beds were all made from natural materials. These guys came here the day after reporting to "reeducation." It was quite true that those reported to District Five received better treatment. My two friends that planned originally to go with me instead went to District Three had been here for nearly a year. One of those who had moved out was Navy Lt. Lê văn Tư whom I met in 1973 in a gathering of officers of Chinese descent in Saigon; he graduated from the well-known Cao Thắng Technical High School where students learned hands-on technical skills. I heard that not too long after the move Tư escaped.

We had the entire day to get acquainted with our living arrangement and I was impressed with what bare hands could accomplish. When the detainees first came they had to sleep on hammocks hung between trees. Using handmade tools, bit by bit they opened up the jungle and even cleared a field for soccer with the tough job of removing the stumps. At the meantime many lots had been prepared for erecting centralized buildings.

In the first evening, drizzle welcomed us in the dark jungle and I felt very downcast. After dinner we sat in the hut illuminated by a tiny kerosene lamp. Some music came from a neighboring hut behind the trees of a stringed instrument playing "Bésame mucho." The two-string instrument was made from a condensed milk can and frog skin. The quản-giáo knew no Western tunes; it was safe as long as we did not sing the lyrics. That tune was the most heard one on the evenings and it was soon superseded by guitars from Long-Khánh when the tiny individual huts were dismantled and we moved to the new houses.

Once in a while, I heard some continuous high-pitched noise from afar. I put my question to an old-timer if there was a lumber mill in this labor camp. No, that was the sound from a species of cicada called bell cicada.

From the next day on, each evening our A came together to receive work assignments from the quản-giáo through the A leader. The assignments varied from gathering bamboos or rattans, cutting trees or cogon grass, even occasionally harvesting bamboo shoots for the common kitchen. Each work assignment had specified quantity and measurement. We worked six days a week and had Sundays off.

Some worked as carpenters primarily producing beds for the quản-giáo who treasured the traditional headboard design of a rising sun with radiating sunbeams. A couple guys including an A-1 Skyraider pilot stood in the sawing pit all day to cut logs into planks.

Four people including Hồ Kim worked in the foundry; they made machetes, sickles, hoes, spades, axes, and chisels from leaf springs, iron rods, even tracks salvaged from a destroyed M41 tank. Our B walked several miles to bring back those track pieces; axes made from the steel tracks were hard and sharp, I had brought one home when I was released. Two older folks manufactured charcoals for the foundry's furnace which was equipped with manually driven piston bellows made from the cannon powder canisters. Only certain tools like saw blades were provided by the camp.

Some weaker buddies stayed close to the huts to take care of the vegetable garden which was fertilized by human wastes from the only latrine in the C twenty feet behind our hut and my bed; vegetable cultivated was solely amaranth or pigweed that grew to six feet tall. We had amaranth soup nearly every day which we called drumstick soup. Hồ Kim,

2nd Lt. Trung and I ate in a group. I proposed to split our rations of rice into three meals: two bowls for breakfast, one each for lunch and dinner; everyone ayed. I drank a lot of water when feeling hungry.

We had to build three new living quarters, a dining hall and an assembly hall. Thanked to the old-timers' efforts we did not need to clear out more lands but gather and prepare the building materials.

I got used gradually to carry weighty stuffs on my shoulders. The bamboo bundle pressing on the shoulder created painful pressure. I was barely able to stand up in my first trial to carry the newly cut cogon grass hung on the two ends of a tree branch. My sickle was so crudely tooled that I had to force it through the grass; the grass blades and the sickle had sawed through my precious clothing and cut my fingers. Getting my hands to bleed a little bit from cuts was a daily thing.

In order to harvest the grass, we went out through a guarded gate, on getting back we had to take off our hats and glasses to request permission. On the back side of the camp the jungle was wide open, we could go as far as needed, yet I had not known anyone tried to escape in that direction.

The original assembly hall where we had taken a few lessons resembled a circular tree house built around a big tree. The tree itself was pockmarked with damages from heavy bombing.

There were many B-52 bomb craters in the Katum jungle, rows of huge round holes filled with crystal-clear water, displaying distinct layers of geological makeup.

This place was a Vietcong stronghold and they knew every nook and cranny. There were vestiges of booby-traps that had been removed then filled up with dirt. Perhaps all landmines had been cleared out for I had not heard of mine accidents in the camp. I bumped into a spot where empty C-rations littered just a few steps from the belowground pipes that dispersed smokes from a field kitchen to avoid detection from air reconnaissance; it must be a close encounter between the Special Forces and Vietcong.

Bamboo

Cutting a bamboo seemed easy and straightforward but could become really dangerous, without using a free hand grasping the bamboo which could become a spring-loaded razor-sharp spear shot up to your face when cut. I learned to be cautious after a near-miss in the first couple days in Katum.

Supposedly all bamboos were straight but not necessary so. After surveying a bamboo from different angles and made certain that it was straight, yet when I pulled it out, it was a zigzag. Occasionally, the bamboos in a cluster were knitted together tightly at the top and we had to leave the hewn ones behind because two people could not yank them free.

The jungle was dark even at high noon due to the thick canopy and dense vegetation. One day working along several guys in the wood, I was searching out a suitable tree and heard a cry of "timber" followed by the loud rustle of a falling tree; lo and behold, the felled tree was blocked from hitting me by a few inches and I was covered with broken twigs and leaves. The guy who felled the tree hurried over and profusely apologized to me.

Moving around in the jungle was not easy especially carrying a heavy load, to conserve energy I tried not to go out too far not to mention of the trouble of getting lost. The jungle had no banana or fruit trees as in the Tarzan movies; the prevalent food supplements we could gather were bamboo shoots or rather the tender tips of young bamboos. When the three of us in the group got time to pick the shoots then we could add to our meal a pound of boiled bamboo tips. We were supposed to eat only what was rationed, fortunately, the quản-giáo did not come to check on us.

Prisoner of War and "Reeducation"

Animal Protein

One day on the edge of our B's vegetable plot I saw a tiny rodent caught by a trap: beneath an arch made from bent bamboo, a mouse was pinned down by a bamboo lever ballasted on the opposite end with a chunk of dried mud.

Somehow, Hồ Kim got a mouse cage trap, so we tried our luck by attaching some rice to the trigger pin as bait. The next morning, it caught a mouse. Kim was not brave enough to kill it, so I played the executioner based on my experience in killing chickens. I killed the poor thing using a sharpened iron rod, there was not much blood shed due to its small size. Its fur was light brown and looked clean; to safeguard against the ticks, I poured boiling water on the carcass. After chopping off its head and paws, I pulled off the skin in one piece and cleaned out the innards. From then on, mice became frequent supplement to our meals.

I became known in the C as the mouse chef. One day when people clearing out a huge pile of lumber, dozens of mouse scurried from their hiding place and some of them got clubbed to death. Twenty mice were brought to me; I cooked and delivered them to those who took part in the hunt. Three of us each had a whole one for that dinner.

Twice, my food allergy flared up after eating the mouse. My upper lip was swollen and because of that I got a day off.

A couple years after arriving in the States, I chatted with a guy who was put in the Chí Hòa prison in Saigon for he was in the Police. According to him, jokingly, that I was too wasteful by then! What they caught were sewer rats and they prepared the whole rodents saving all their internal organs and even the skins through careful shaving. The environment was so restrictive they could not roam freely. In the past, a prison cell used to hold ten convicts, now forty to fifty detainees; therefore everyone sat in their underwear during the day. People tried to supplement their diet with some green; the yard in which they were let out during the day became barren in a few months after all the grass been eaten. He would not go to the zoo any longer for the cages reminded him of the painful past.

Similarly, I would stay away from two things: camping and cruise ship (after the "boat people" experience).

Jungle Pests

In the jungle, mosquitoes swarmed around the bamboos; leeches and their smaller cousins the land leeches occupied the damp places; ticks waiting for their next hosts behind dried leaves and rotten trees.

I found a leech on my leg after sensing coldness down below by then the bloodsucker had already finished its banquet; I plucked it out and smudged it on the ground, there was no time to try out the traditional wisdom of using saliva to dislodge a clinging leech. After a leech applied its powerful blood thinner and blood kept flowing from the wound for a while even after it was removed. Despite not the tiny ticks, they hid behind the earlobes or in the private areas. We learned of their presence only by the ensuing fever and careful checking. I was sickened once by a tick lodged behind my ear.

Several times I saw small emerald pythons hanging down from tree branches; and a white-and-yellow snake curling beneath a rotting stump. Besides our crude machetes we always carried a one-meter long rattan cane for measurement and to whack the snakes.

On a bamboo shoot harvesting trip I bumped into a 500- or 750-pound bomb with fins attached resting almost flat on the jungle floor atop some shrubs; softly I walked away from that place. Several months later, one night the bomb blew up in a scheduled blaze to clear the land for planting rice; after an earth-shaking explosion a thick fragment of the bomb in the size of a hubcap landed fifty yards from our hut. How destructive it must be when hundreds of these bombs falling from the sky in a B-52 bombing run!

We had no plants similar to poison ivy in the jungle, but we were warned about the lacquer trees. One guy inadvertently brought back a lacquer tree in a bundle for rafters and he was swollen from head to toe for a week. The lacquer tree was orange in color and emitting irritating odor once it was hacked, but lack of experience induced big trouble.

A few times I was permitted to stay behind when I was having a relapse of malaria or when my feet were swollen. I had no problem to deal with malaria for I had brought along my Fansidar, just took three pills and pretty soon I was back to normal. A former Ranger in the next A with chronic malaria had a relapse and he was nursed back to health by his older brother's spoon-feeding.

One job that was available inside the camp for the sick was putting the cogon grass into clips. The grasses were dried under the sun for a few days and we put small bundles of them between four slats of bamboo in a sequential order; if the procedure was not followed exactly, all the grasses would fall off. Our hut required more than a thousand clips of grass for the roof. Supposedly the thatched roof could last a decade.

One day when I was squatting on the rafters to latch the grass clips onto the roof, blood from my hemorrhoids dripped to the ground below. I was relieved from that kind of squatting job from then on.

Besides the nails that were made from barbed wires all the other fasteners we used came from nature. We went to work carrying only machetes or sickles. We tied up the bamboos or tree limbs with vines, bundled the cut grass with hand-twisted grass ropes. Bedframes and doorframes came together in dovetails, bamboo strips tied down to the bedframes by sliced rattans. Our carpenters made our beds very sturdy and comfortable. The rafters, thatches, and woven bamboo panels were bound by vines or finely split bamboo laces.

On sick days I did light work of weaving bamboo panels which were widely used for wall and window and grain storage in Asia. Newly cut bamboos were put in the pond till they produced a very unpleasant smell, then we split them into thin slabs and wove into panels. I guessed that the soaking produced an odorous compound that could deter insects and prolong the useful life of the panels.

Due to the seriousness of my hemorrhoids I was exempted from moving logs. It took eight to ten guys to carry one on shoulder, the freshly cut trees were very heavy with sap and people had to get the big trees quite far off. Many trees were cut and brought back for benches in the assembly hall; we stripped out the barks and used machetes or axes to smooth out long flat surfaces to sit on.

Fortunately our B did not take part in erecting the upper structure of the assembly hall which was fifteen meters high at the apex. There was an organized competition among the Cs for the tallest hall. One day, in another C, some guys were working in their hall, the structure collapsed and one was crushed to death. If this happened during the day of assembly, casualties might be in the hundreds. According to some, due to the shortage of tall trees, some pillars that were a bit short therefore did not set to the required depth led to the structural failure.

Once or twice a month, we came together to knock off the barks from the logs with wooden clubs or metal tools. To bring some spice to life I imagined the poundings sounded like African jungle drumbeats in Tarzan movies.

In Katum there was no lack of firewood and we could boil water or cook as much as we needed to. Our common fireplaces were made out of a shallow pit under two barbed wire posts. Since matches were precious, tinder boxes were maintained day and night. With plenty of bamboos and access to fire, many flutes were made.

Many went to the fireplace in the chilly mornings to enjoy their water pipes. Tobacco for pipes was very strong and could make people especially with empty stomach getting high speedily. One guy in another C had a fainting spell after inhaling, he struggled to prop himself up with his hand not to fall into the fire pit, his charred hand was amputated!

Morning Exercise

After moving into our new huts with the wide open yards, the morning exercise began. Five in the morning, at the sound of a gong we gathered in the yard for a ten- to fifteen-minute exercise. Some people were picked to lead the exercise; when it was my turn, three quarters down the routine I had to be reminded of the next move and that was my first and last turn. What a relief!

One day I was working in the carpenter shop, I whistled "The Long and Winding Road" by the Beatles and it caught the attention of Đặng Trung Tâm. He came over and befriended me, for not that many were fond of Western music. Tâm was short with a lot of facial and body hairs; he was known as "Tâm the shorty" or Tâm Lùng in Vietnamese and his name was transposed to that of Tùng Lâm a famous comedian.

When there was another shuffling within the C, Tâm moved over taking up the spot of Hồ Kim who was assigned to the foundry group's corner; so we had opportunities to reminisce the nightclubs and Rock bands in Saigon. During the night whenever I woke up, I could hear the screeching noise of Tâm grinding his teeth. In daytime hours Tâm was a happy guy cracking jokes all the time, but beneath the façade he was like everyone else being eaten up by worries and hopelessness.

After nightfall, before the 9:00 p.m. curfew there was not much to do in the huts with a few kerosene lamps. We gathered in small groups to talk about our past and families. Quite frequently some gathered in the adjacent hut to listen to live music. Sanh, the fighter-bomber pilot turned carpenter, with a tremendous voice would sing some Vietnamese melodies with guitar accompaniment. A sentinel was posted to watch out the quản-giáo. One of the pre-1950s songs which I did not know touched me very deeply. It was called Thuyền Viễn Xứ—The Ship Far Away from Hometown; the tune befitted the sentiment of those who had lost everything. Its lyrics were:

> This evening smoky mist rises
> Setting sun touches the pier
> Reddish clouds mix in with twilight
> Riding the waves of the Black River, a ship sails abroad
> O ship leaves home of old
> Once more brushes past the sparse reeds
> Hey, the singing for a thousand years
> Home fountain far off and silent, the afternoon rains return
>
> Refrain:
> Look toward the home path, hometown so far away
> Sad pace of life falters
> My steps stumble
> Look back to the direction of the village
> Tears of the Black River thick
> Old mama sits with silhouette immobile
> Her hairs snowy white
> Her expecting heart frail
>
> This evening I send to my old homeland
> Innumerable homesick thoughts
> High sky glides down to earth
> Countless sorrow on foreign soil
> Thick and smoky mist rises up
> Willows swing on the river bank
> This evening by the quay of the four winds
> A ship far from home lifts anchor and sets sail...

Prisoner of War and "Reeducation"

This song came out when the South and North were divided in 1954 by the Geneva Accords. Many favorite songs during the Vietnam War were off-limits, so we played only those that were not politically incorrect.

There were remarkable things happened in our hut. A guy whose bed set diagonally to mine named Huỳnh văn Đức, an Ensign; he was always pale since I met him. One day, after finishing my assignment I sat on my bed, for we were not allowed to lie down in daytime hours, but Đức was quietly lying on his bed sick. Our doctor Nghĩa came and put his ear over Đức's chest to listen to Đức's weakening heartbeat. Nghĩa stood up and shook his head. At that moment a soldier came in, he took from his shirt pocket an acupuncture needle and thrusted it into Đức's philtrum did a few twirls; a dying Đức came back to life!

Under its thick canopy the jungle was cold in the morning and the evening; therefore usually we took our baths in the early afternoon after finishing our works not to get a cold, for no one had towels to dry ourselves. The well water was quite cold and I used to take my bath very quickly just rubbing off the sweat and dirt. After coming back to life, at first Đức said that he saw the Virgin Mary but later on the Buddha. In order to meet this "divine" person he had to be clean therefore bathed at four in the morning. Instead of getting sick by the cold baths he was getting stronger day by day.

Later, Đức and I had individually got some transcendental meditation lessons from a buddy under the same roof. This fellow was kind and soft-spoken; he taught us to take the lotus position, meditate, and mantra chant inside the mosquito net at midnight. By keeping the mind clear from all the worldly struggles; gradually the soul would leave the body to a heavenly realm, the higher one go up the more one would learn the deep teachings of Buddha. There were many spirits around us trying to steal our merits to attain nirvana sooner; but there was a provision of safeguard, a protector called Ông

Tám or Eighth Elder who would come to the rescue when we called on his name. After trying out for a week and going nowhere but deprived me of sleep, I gave up the whole thing.

One day, each of us got distributed a piece of camouflage-patterned fabric measuring one meter by two meter as blankets; those were fabrics for the uniforms of ARVN Airborne and Rangers. Since my blanket was still in good shape, and the nylon hat had been battered, therefore I modeled after the old hat and sewed a wide brim one.

Our C had new arrivals from Hóc Môn, they were Captains. Each camp with its peculiar surroundings came up with special musical instruments. From Long-Khánh we made guitars of plywood; these came from an Engineer Corps' base with lots of aluminum and they brought along saxophones, flutes, and the unheard-of aluminum violins.

One day a new guy with big fat belly was walking to his hut after bathing, wearing only his shorts. I heard a guard called to his pal to look at the pregnant man! In the poverty-stricken North they did not have that many chubby men around.

The Captains brought news about our female counterparts, the ARVN Women Auxiliary Corps Officers. The housing for the WACs was adjacent to the Captains'; many of them brought their children even newborns along because their husbands reported to "reeducation" at the same time. It was heart-wrenching to hear those moms caring for their young in such calamitous conditions, and sadder tales of some had to compromise with their male captors. These women suffered much more than men.

Paving Road

After another round of political lessons in the new hall, we began to build a road for visitation. The section we worked on had had logs lined up horizontally as roadbed, we dug up the dirt and put on top of the logs to the height of one meter.

One day I saw 2nd Lt. Trần Minh Khiếu of the Second Ambulance Company from afar, we waved to each other vigorously. Our eyesight was quite good in picking out friends from a distance even though we all looked like beggars. On another occasion, I saw Lương Tô while we were walking to the worksite; we waved with big smile, he looked just as strong as I could recall a taekwondo black belt.

The visiting time had come. Supposedly we were to inform our families not to bring in much food for we were treated well, but the outside world knew better. From the beginning, large amount of goodies had been brought in.

It was my turn for the visitation. Anna with Mary our daughter, Mom and my eldest brother Ju-Hua were waiting for me in the visitors' shed. My youngest brother Ju-Xiang could not get in due to the quota of three. It was the first time seeing my daughter who was a wobbling baby of year and half. Mary was propped up on the bamboo table by Anna, I opened wide my arms but she would not go to a stranger. There were snacks and soft drinks on the table but I did not feel like eating and drinking only eagerly absorbed all the news: many people had successfully fled the country by boat, our family was not in a desperate situation to take the risk for we had the hope of legally immigrating to the States and was able to stay put due to the pig farm being counted as a farming activity.

When I reported for "reeducation" I had carried my civilian ID card and here in Katum the quản-giáo once threatened to inspect our belongings to see if we still had document from the "Counterfeit" regime. We brought our bags and spread out the contents in the yard for inspection, confidently I kept my ID card in the pocket. This time I handed my ID to my brother. Today I still have the card.

It took my family two days to come to this secluded place; they hired all means of transportation like three-wheeled scooter, motorbike taxis and logging truck to come to the camp.

Scattered outside the camp was a New Economic Zone with thatch huts and people in rags. Mom's hairs grayed so much compared to that in my memory. Everyone wore sandals.

The visit lasted only half an hour and the guards came to dismiss us. My most intimate gesture to Anna was holding her hands. For the visit the Lambretta scooter had been sold to bring me 150 pounds of foodstuff. My family had cooked me a chicken which turned rancid after the steamy two-day journey, Mom and Anna advised me to throw it away for the sake of health.

My friends helped to bring in the baskets of food. I was hesitating if the chicken should be trashed, Lê văn Thanh, the school teacher, said that it was unthinkable to do that and we had nothing to lose even if we die from food poisoning! So he stir-fried the chicken thoroughly for a long time. We had a chicken feast in spite of a faintly rancid taste and nobody got sick from that.

I got sixty pounds of cane sugar squares alone, plus cooking oil, peanuts, red beans, mung beans, fluffy dried pork, and powdered rice. Some of these were considered contrabands but the guards never inspected what we had gotten.

Like the soldiers in the POW camps the guards here privately expressed their view that some people especially families of officers were so well-off in the South while they were dirt poor in the North. People up North had firmly believed that they had to live on subsistence for the righteous cause of liberating people in the South struggling under the vise of the Counterfeit Regime and the American Imperialists; they bit a grain of rice into two to share it with the Southern people. One thing the guards did not know was that people in the South had been selling off what they had from bicycles, motorbikes, watches, refrigerators, televisions, furniture, even garments, to the "liberators".

After receiving the food aids, I got used to pop a couple of sugar squares in my mouth when feeling hungry. I treated the inner circle with sweet soups which I put in a whole pound of sugar for my sweet tooth. Some wondered about my extravagant use of sugar while others used only a few sugar squares. My rationale was that I did not know when I would die or things might be taken away or how to manage the heavy load when we had to move again.

For the visitation, some got small packages and some had no visitors.

Some families brought in live chickens and Hồ Kim got a cock. A chicken house was built by the side of our hut. There were plenty of termites in the jungle and the chicken owners brought back sections of the rock-hard mounds to feed the chicks with termite larvae. One day while Kim was working in the foundry, someone gathered two cocks for a fight and Kim's cock got blinded in one eye. Hồ Kim was so furious that he swore to kill the culprit once he found it out.

One day, I stood on my bed poking my hand into the storage rack under the roof, suddenly my arm was jabbed by something burning and it turned out to be from a big bad scorpion. My arm got swollen at once but was not very painful.

Châu Thế Mưu was a 2nd Lt. in the Fifth Army Division; his father owned a department store which was the sole agent of the Bic ballpoint pens. Mưu got money from the family visit in addition to those huge baskets; he and his friends went all the way to the New Economic Zone village to buy moonshine rice wine.

A guy spread the news that he encountered panthers in the wood, he meant the ARVN Rangers with the insignia of a panther, but no one showed any interest. Firstly, a few ARVN soldiers could not survive or fight in the jungle; secondly, it could be a trap for the simpleton. We heard that a guy suspected to be an informant was killed in the wood.

Graveyard in the Jungle

One day, Hồ Kim told me the shocking news of the death of Lương Tô who died from digestive issues after the family visit.

The next Sunday, Kim and I went to a small burial plot containing several dirt mounds. We identified Tô's tomb by a crude wooden grave marker with his name, dates of birth and death. Hồ Kim recounted that before Tô was put in the coffin, people stuffed his mouth with rice powder so that he would not go hungry on the journey to the netherworld. I stood there gripped by strong emotions about his sad ending and the despondency of our own. We could not stay there too long because the place was quite far away.

New Year Celebration

It was almost lunar New Year of 1977, a lot of festivities had been planned. An evening of celebration was scheduled and we were encouraged to compose new songs for thanking and praising the Party and the Government. I joined one of the two choruses and spent several evenings in practice. One of the songs was a tune written in the pre-War period recounting the glory of Vietnam. A new song composed by a guy graduated from the National Conservatory; his tune was tasteless sounded like those pre-1975 tunes for ballroom dancing. In contrast, there was a song written by a young guy, he was one of the Đà Lạt Military Academy cadets got hastily commissioned in the remaining days of South Vietnam; since they were officers therefor had to be "reeducated." His song carried a lively tune, beside the compulsory theme of praising socialism and "labor is glorious", it reminded me of our life by then, it was tinged with sadness only an insider could sense:

> Thousands of flowers smile shyly to greet the new spring,
> Spring of peace and happiness chants songs of tranquility,
> Spring is new so are the people,

Labor in this spring, full stomach and warmth for the ensuing thousand days.
Here're the hoe strokes, we hoe really deep,
Change this arid land into greenish good soil.
Thousands of smiling people cheering on socialism,
Spring of peace and happiness chants songs of tranquility,
Spring anew and people renewed,
Labor in this spring, full stomach and warmth for the following thousand generations.
Here's the power of life, the strength of both hands,
Transform this sheet of thatch to a warm roof for the long night.

La, la, la...

 Hồ Kim was to prepare a lion dance for the celebration. We had a few guys who had been involved in martial arts groups in Cholon but they rather let me join hands with Hồ Kim to construct a lion head. So with bamboo twigs we tried to make one, but due to our inexperience the head turned out to be big and unwieldy. Using several colors of paint we tried our best on the lion head. For the body of the lion we tagged on a piece of camouflaged cloth. We cut in half a fifty-five gallon fuel drum as our drum and the foundry gang made a gong and cymbals. No one volunteered to be the drummer, since I liked to play the lion dance drum since fourth grade so I filled in.
 During the New Year celebration our lion dance troupe were permitted the rare opportunity to visit an adjacent C. I did not plan to play the entire gamut including kung fu performances. A buddy, looked like had taken some rice wine, when hearing my drum beats for martial arts, he walked into the open space and began his show, quite abruptly he stopped cold in his movement after sensing a warning stare from an onlooker.

During this festival we got a large piece of pork, about half pound each with skin and fat; it was not free though, each one paid one piaster in the new currency, equivalent to the old 500 piasters. Nobody tried to finish the meat in one pass but saved some for the next day. There was a rumor that some C was visited by an international delegation and for this occasion people there had pork plus fried eggrolls! The delegation gave a talk, when it came to the Q&A, no one spoke up. The speaker said that he knew that we had been treated "well" by the Government. The rumor, unconfirmed up to this day, gave us a flimsy hope that we were still under the watchful eyes of the international community.

House Fire

One late evening, one of our C's three houses was ignited accidentally. When awakened by the commotion and saw the flames already engulfed the house, we hurriedly prepared to run away with our simple belongings, for all the houses were close by. The house was quickly destroyed. A few days later, that B moved elsewhere.

Planting Rice

After the New Year break, we were to prepare for rice planting in the Montagnard way of slash-and-burn. All the able-bodied were mobilized. The sharpest tools available were a limited number of axes made from the tank tracks therefore we could not cut the trees flush to the ground. On the lands that had been cleared, we inched our way to shun the pointy stumps.

We were there for more than a year now and the jungle had been opened up quite a bit. One day while taking a break we heard noises from a distance around a tall tree. I thought those guys must be excited to watch the tree tumbling down. A few minutes later the tree did fall and there were cheers. It turned out that a wager was going on: one kilogram of sugar on whether one could fell that tree with one hundred axe strokes. The tree was still standing after all the strokes, but after swinging back and forth for a while finally it went crashing down.

The burning took about a week, after the ground cooled down we gingerly walked through the charred territory and found many spots were yet intact. Now the opened area was ready for planting. We poked holes in the ground roughly a hand span apart and put a few seeds in. Out of frustration I talked to my companions: "What will we get out of this way of rice planting?" Suddenly, from the rear came the voice of a quản-giáo: "That man over there, what had you just said?" I almost had a heart attack! The quản-giáo walked away without any further comments.

I envisaged a gathering of the C in the evening and I was called out for criticism followed by severe punishment. It was a really bad day. I kept blaming myself for my stupidity. Nothing happened that evening or the next day or the next week. I learned another lesson.

A few weeks later there were sporadic bursts of artillery at night, and gradually the blasts got more constant and closer. Finally, we knew the bombardments came from their comrades the Khmer Rouge. We had to move.

We were told to destroy all the vegetable gardens; Hồ Kim and I were assigned to tear down two plots of yam. The plants were not old enough to have tubers, but we would not waste their leaves, so we gathered them to boil a large pot and consumed them all. Next day in the latrine all those extra fiber gave me big trouble.

A couple days before the move, we had a mission to bring back some manioc stems.

The manioc or cassava was a very robust tuberous plant which would grow by simply staking a section of the stem into the ground. Cassava was the mainstay of Vietcong in the jungle; neither slashing nor fires from napalm could destroy all the tubers underground. The manioc tuber especially its purplish rind contained cyanogenic glucosides which caused my gum to swell; even when I was very hungry I would not eat them. Fortunately, we were fed cassava only a few times. I watched some buddies, who salvaged the discarded cassava rinds, through rinsing, soaking, boiling, turned them into a treat. If one was caught picking the tender leaves of manioc for soup would be punished. (Small bundles of cassava leaves were available in some supermarkets in the States; they reminded me of the hard times in the labor camp.)

This trip was a trek to a New Economic Zone village twenty kilometers away. When we were in the Thủ Đức OCS we had a one-day trek before graduation. We carried a knapsack loaded with ammunition, rations, a foldaway spade, one half of a canvas tent, and a poncho. We trekked on an open plain; we were well-fed and expecting to be knighted as an officer. This time, the troop was half-starved, dispirited, walked through the jungle and escorted by armed guards.

The destination spot was swarmed with a small army of the village kids selling foodstuffs. We bought candies and snacks from them. There were heaps of manioc stems and each one carried a bundle. The trip took about six hours.

Then it was the moving day. We collected our belongings and boarded a convoy. We had no idea where we were heading, hopefully not as labor-intensive as this one.

The convoy trundled for five, six hours and was climbing. Some guessed that we were on the Hồ Chí Minh trail. I dozed off on the bench suddenly a strong breeze flipped up a corner of the canvas canopy and my new cone hat from Anna got sucked out of the truck and flew away.

From the forest, a stag ran across the road in front of us and the truck stopped at once, two guards rushed out with AK-47's excitedly yelling and chasing after the deer but it was too late, it went into the wood.

Camp Bù Gia Mập

Finally the convoy came to a stop. We disembarked and were herded down a hollow with gentle decline. After crossing a bridge of big logs we saw a u-shaped cluster of houses, which were made out of bamboos. The bamboos we had in Katum were the size of the big toes and here they were the size of our legs. These houses were taller than the ones we just left behind and the roof was also of bamboo.

We were in Phước-Long Province in the region called Bù Gia Mập or Sóc Bom Bo, the place name that we heard frequently from a song.

The compound was half-circled by a stream about ten feet wide, therein we were to bathe, wash, and swim. About a week later, one guy in our C caught a big fish just by planting a fishing line and a handmade hook. The news spread through the whole place and everyone was excited that there was fish even in this mountain brook. The fish weighed at least five pounds.

There I met Lư Tô who was supposed to report for "reeducation" with me. There was not much to do in this place, therefore life was relatively easy.

Someone was clearing out weeds around the camp, and his hoe struck a M79 grenade, the explosion knocked him out. In order to clean the head wound his hairs were shorn. In the evening he kept vomiting and people worried that he might die; after much convulsion a tapeworm came out from his mouth. Eventually he recovered.

Some went in the bamboo forest picking the huge bamboo shoots and sun-dried them as present in future family visit. I tried hard to scout the bamboo bushes but could not even locate one single shoot.

We were supplied twice with flour to make bread. Our chefs scavenged a few old fuel drums and transformed them into bread ovens. We were fed bo bo or sorghum a few times and chewed really hard in order to swallow them. When we fed this tasteless and coarse staple to the pigs, they refused to eat them.

One day on the dirt road, without escorting guards, we bumped into a band of Montagnards walked on the other side of the road in single file. One of us probed them in English: "V.C. number one?" Quite unexpectedly a man among them responded: "Number ten!" We were so hilarious everybody laughed and soon enough the anecdote was broadcasted all over the camp.

Trương Kỳ Minh, a graduate of journalism from Đà Lạt College. He was tall, well-built and practiced kung fu; people nicknamed him "Minh vồ" i.e. Minh with a protruding forehead. In Katum, we had a few opportunities to chat about the Taoist way of healthy living not to open one's mouth while bathing to prevent getting a cold, the ancient exercises imitating eight different insects.

One day Minh approached me to see if I would skip camp with him and walk to Thailand through Cambodia. He showed me a dagger Hồ Kim had wrought for him. Without hesitation, I told him that it was too risky along with so many unknowns. He said that he had made up his mind in predicting no opportunity being released, so he would rather fight to the end.

A couple days later, the gong sounded and we were gathered to hear the announcement of absence and presumed escape of Minh. Nothing had been heard about him since. Prior to this not too long ago, a couple guys skipped camp and pretty soon they were paraded before us in bounds caught by the Border Patrols. I felt sad for Minh, not like the idiomatic saying that no news was good news, when there was no news about him that meant he was no more.

The Last Visit

Another family visitation time, and this round the families were permitted to stay overnight. This time, Anna left our daughter at home and came with my brothers.

Far away from the gate that crowded with visiting families I spotted one woman in bright orange dress standing out in a throng of drab visitors. I was wondering who would in her right mind wear that kind of clothing for this was no occasion for wedding party. The lady turned out to be my wife! I told her that I did not want to attract too much attention in this place. Anna said that she got no decent clothes for the visitation, so when she was given the cloth remnant from a neighbor she made it into a new dress by hand. In order to prevent unplanned pregnancy that happened to so many other visiting wives, my parents required that my brothers slept next to us that night. Some women remained in the forest after the visit by staying in tree houses from bamboos. Some children were born while the fathers were still in captivity.

Although it was a whole day visit but it was too short for all of us. Anna and my brothers reiterated the hardship and difficulties for the chartered van climbing the rolling hills and going through a flooded valley. Mosquitoes were so numerous in that place that one could kill dozens of them attacking his butt in the latrine even during daytime.

There came up a female dentist to visit her family; she brought along dental tools and offered extraction and minor dental works to the detainees.

Camp Doctor

The atmosphere in the camp got very excited when the doctors, pharmacists and some others categories of detainees obtained a one-month home leave. During that period, three guys and I were picked to become "camp doctors". We handed out analgesics, put iodine tincture on abrasions and bandaged minor injuries. One of us had been a nursing officer and he did the injections. The few syringes and needles we had inherited were the disposable ones. To prepare for injection, we boiled the plastic syringes for a few minutes trying not to destroy the rubber stoppers. The needle points were bent and dull after much use so our nursing officer used all his skills to bring them back to usable shape on a tiny whetstone.

It was hilarious when the guys returned with two extreme cases of transformation. A physician in my hut came back morphed into a ruddy chubby fellow having gained at least ten kilos. The guy that caught the fish from the stream used to be quite muscular became very skinny after he went on a month-long honeymoon.

Leaving Camp

A month later, on January 15, 1978, I was released along with all the medical personnel. Our release papers were signed by a Major General. My paper indicated that I had to report to the People's Committee of Lái Thiêu (based on the release application my family put in for me). Each of us also received some money for bus fare. I ran about the camp and bid farewell to all the folks that I knew.

We walked away from the gate in the afternoon with our dinners. I wore my hand-sewn wide rim hat, on my back was an Australian knapsack holding my clothing and hand-sewn handbag plus an axe made by the Katum foundry from tank track; on my feet were U.S. blue deck shoes. The sack and shoes were from an open market in Saigon for the recent visit.

What a taste of freedom. The air was fresh, the sky was blue, and everything appeared so lovely!

We walked the several miles gleefully and raucously till we came to a wooden shed by the roadside where we stayed for the night. The next day we went to a long-distance bus station, and bought tickets. The first thing I noticed from the bus which I had not experienced from that of the military trucks was the odor of the fume, it smelled like rotten egg, from the gasoline of the Big Soviet Brother. The trip took nearly ten hours but felt more like an hour or two. We bade farewell to each other at the Seven Corners terminal and went our own way. I enquired about the fare and hopped on a motorbike taxi and in twenty minutes I was home.

Saigon had changed ... drastically! On the streets, traffic was relatively sparse to what I could recall. Besides the military vehicle and public transportation there were some sedans, motorbikes were definitely outnumbered by bicycles. All the concrete buildings looked grayish with dust and soot; many walls had big blackened holes which I realized were vents for the wood stoves. There were many soldiers walking among the people. People on the streets were not in better clothes than ours in the camps, they looked haggardly. It was the sequel of "Street without Joy."

Chapter 5.

Boat People and Refugee Camps

The freshness of freedom and family reunion evaporated very rapidly. The next day I reported to the Public Security of the block and was told to report instead to that of Bình Dương as stated on the release paper. Dad's business partner of the pig farm contacted the Bình Dương authority and that did not work out either. The place that required no residential document was the New Economic Zone.

Five weeks after my return, Anna was in the family way.

Another Hemorrhoid Surgery
Soon enough, my hemorrhoids acted up again and bled seriously, I needed another operation. We found Dr. La Đồng Ký who was also recently released and working in the former Chiang Kai-Shek or Trung Chính Hospital. He operated on me with a surgical team all of whom were of the former epoch. The astounding things I saw were the surgical gloves which had been re-used many times; their brownish crispy appearance reminded me of the cicada shells. I could not imagine how the surgical team operated with such things. Fortunately they still had the anesthetics for the epidural.

On the eve before my surgery, Anna and I were chatting on the balcony, there came loud voices from the intake room downstairs. A woman was embracing her husband and kept yelling to him to hang on in a diabetic coma. Not that long afterwards the yelling changed to wailing when he died. No more insulin for the diabetics.

At Wit's End

After a period of convalescence, we went to see Dr. Ký's father to get a peek into the future. In his courtyard, I prayed to the onlooker spirits and got a number out of a bunch of bamboo sticks. The resulted poem was not clear to answer our question in mind. Mr. La told us to be patient.

Mr. La knew me since I was a teen. He was a teacher turned businessman and learned herbal medicine through self-study. Since many male teachers were plagued by hemorrhoids therefore he improvised an herbal ointment to ameliorate the discomfort. His ointment worked on many people but not on this stubborn case of mine. He jokingly called me "statesman" which in Cantonese sounded as "man with authentic hemorrhoids." Mr. La used to provide me some ointment in tin tubes to alleviate my problem. Even Dr. Ký, now in Canada, used his father's ointment to treat some less serious cases or to prevent the recurrence of hemorrhoid after surgery.

Some years ago, Mr. La bought a worn-out booklet called "Kong-Ming Fortunes" from a curbside stand. Kong-Ming was a legendary figure renowned for his military and political wisdom in the Three Kingdoms Period around 250 AD. The booklet contained 384 poems based on the combinations of Taoist "eight trigrams", deciphering these poems would provide answers to issues of life.

After the disastrous withdrawal from the Central Highlands, my family got bits and pieces of bad news that I got stuck on the Interprovincial Route Seven B. Desperate to find out whether I was dead or alive, my eldest brother

Ju-Hua went to see Mr. La. The poem came up numbered 215 read:

> Hilly paths deem easy too
> Amidst clouds flies lonely goose
> Peach blossom under sudden showers
> By riverbank young lady cowers

Mr. La deciphered the poem and comforted my brother that I was going through serious problems yet would come home in one piece, with a girl. Through that my family held on a glimmer of hope expecting to see me alive after the ordeal and somewhat prepared psychologically to see a woman by my side.

In Hiding
Public Security of the block inquired where I was, Anna said that I was working in the pig farm but they knew no place would accept me except the NEZ, so they came to check me out. As before 1975 the National Police would raid homes for draft dodgers, now the Public Security would come and seek me out. The raids were carried out at night; the first time I climbed over to the neighbor's home and hid behind a water tank. But this could be easily seen, so we came up with an in-house hideout. We emptied out one of the three partitions of a cupboard in the living room for me to curl up inside. Surely the Public Security came again and I hid inside the cupboard when the door bell was rung. While they were checking out each of the three floors, I was worrying whether the thin cupboard bottom could withstand my weight without cracking or making noise to give out my presence.

It was not safe to stay home anymore, I had to go somewhere. My parents tried all they could to send me out first, if I could reach the free world then the three of us would reunite afterwards, but Anna was suspicious that it could be a plot to get rid of her and Mary, so the situation became very awkward and tense.

Before the Communist takeover, my parents did not invest in gold but had all the money in the bank for business transactions. While we took no stock in gold, some families accumulated much through the years. Some families had enough gold to send all their children out even pay their way out of prison when caught.

Due to the difficulties of earning a living in this harsh environment, cheating became common practice, especially in the matters of fleeing the country by boat. Tales of treachery were not news anymore. Desperately, my parents were trying hard to ship me out. So I went to stay in the home of Dad's cousin for two weeks and I heard the organizer talked about the planning of going from Cholon to a Mekong Delta location. The thing turned out to be fictitious but we had nothing to lose.

In the middle of 1978, there was news that the Public Security in the ports of Vũng Tàu and Biên Hòa were accepting gold for outgoing boats. Buddy Châu Thế Muru who was released a short time after me, came and described such a boat that would sail to Hong Kong, onboard there were plenty of water and food, the cost for each passenger was fifteen taels of gold.

A couple months later, from Hong Kong came Muru's letter: he had reached the safe haven.

Not long after that Hồ Kim came and talked about his plan to flee through Phan Thiết which was further out between Vũng Tàu and Nha Trang. I told him that I had no gold.

After we came to the States, I guessed that Muru would resettle in the Western Hemisphere, if he was not qualified to come to the States, then he would likely be in Canada where his late brother had been; I wrote to the Red Cross but they could not locate him.

When the Internet became available, my searches for old friends all came up nothing until a few months before September 11, 2001. I bumped into the phone number of Muru in Frankfurt, Germany; I called him up and learned something about his family, finally I asked him about Hồ Kim. He told me that Kim was killed in the boat trip: his ship encountered Thai pirates, besides the loss of belongings, the females were molested and all the males were stabbed and pushed overboard. Kim's wife and children settled in California and still kept in touch with Muru.

Tales of horrific tragedies abound concerning the "boat people"; many boats went down to the bottom of the South China Sea due to natural and human causes.

China-Vietnam Conflict

When the conflict between Hanoi and Beijing was escalating, lots of Chinese were ready to go back to China through the land routes. Presumably by a scheme of Hanoi to diminish the threat of the million-strong Chinese in the country, a northbound migration was set in motion. We too did prepare to do it during the hype. I taught Anna to write her name in simplified Chinese to show that she was a Chinese. By careful advices from others our plan was scrapped; for it made no sense to flee from one communist regime to submit to another. After going through dangers and hardships, thousands of these returnees still lived in the poor and remote region of China decades later. (The hand of the Lord prevented us in taking another foolish move!)

A Glimmer of Hope

By September, a glimmer of hope appeared. A former employee of Dad had a distant relative Mr. Đăng who was organizing an outgoing boat, and his relative knew someone could help us to get on board! This person—Mr. Yee used to be in the building materials business, he had much gold to lend to people. Since Dad was an established businessman and had a son living in Maryland, so a deal was struck. The costs for us three plus that of the middleman's teenage son came to thirty two taels of gold. The amount of gold we borrowed were thirty five taels, then valued at five thousand dollars; all I had to do was to sign an IOU. (Mr. Yee and his family resettled in Canada and we kept connected for many years until his passing. Mr. Yee confided to me that out of the many families he had lent gold, including his own brothers, I was the only one that paid him back; he returned my IOU note. Praise the Lord for a good conscience to keep my promise.)

In order to stay clear from our home district Public Security, I went to stay in the bakery of the boat organizer Mr. Đăng in Saigon. The bakery was no more in business but it was safe, for the Public Security there was friendly to Mr. Đăng. I slept on the fermentation rack on the second floor and fortunately there were no bed bugs. Staying there also with me was a gray-haired gentleman Mr. Lục who came only after nightfall. Mr. Lục used to be a watch dealer in the prestigious business locale known as Passage d'Eden or Corridor of Eden, and his children would be joining our boat. Mr. Lục lost his home in the "Accounting Operation" through which the government confiscated properties and homes of the capitalist/bourgeois and sent them to the NEZ. During my hiding in Saigon my family was fortunate to have gone through the Operation intact. During that period young workers stayed in the targeted homes to investigate everything in and out, including what was on the dining table. Many families were vacated and forced to the NEZ. People sneaked back to the city after tasting the cruel reality; they had no home to return to just wandered around during daytime and slept on sidewalks after dark. It was one of the reasons people risked all to flee. The Communist used all means to squeeze out the livelihood of those were not on its side.

Mr. Đăng and his grown-up children scrambled around to equip the boat; by taking up the task, the Đăng's got free passage under the auspice of the Public Security. The family consisted of thirty plus souls. They purchased a newly built ocean-going trawler which was twenty five meters long, six meters wide. Because ship engines were in short supply, they bought a Cummings generator. Additionally, they got two Japanese Yanmar outboard motors with extended propeller shafts as auxiliaries.

The Đặng family was really excited to spread the news that the test voyage of the new ship was a success. They contracted a former freighter captain as the pilot, and had gotten a navigational compass from an open air market. The ship was ready to go!

During the stay in the bakery, someone offered me a simple way in treating the frequent swelling of my feet: pig feet soup. To me the idea was ridiculous; how could such an unscientific folk remedy overcome the problem that corticosteroids could not?

Anna was still suspicious of me leaving her and Mary behind after much assurance from me and my parents. On one afternoon after persuading Mom and obtained the address she came to visit me. Her belly was big already. Although having no idea how to deliver a baby, I asked her to prepare scissors, threads and bandages just in case the baby should come out on the boat, hopefully some older ladies might provide help.

For good luck, Mr. Đặng picked 333 as the number for the boat. So our boat bore the registration number VT333. VT stood for Vũng Tàu, commonly known as Cắp, the simplified Cap Saint Jacques.

Every afternoon Mr. Đặng came to the bakery and brought me out to the corner café to have a café latte and a bowl of noodle with dumplings; that was the time I had eaten the most Cantonese dumplings in my whole life.

The evening before the departure, I was asked to type up a roster of the boat. I was a little bit amazed by the name list, because this kind of boat trip commonly known as "Open Exit" was supposedly reserved for Chinese, but many were Vietnamese, therefore, it was not ethnicity that counted but gold did the talking. Hanoi plotted the exodus of Chinese to minimize the threat and to scoop up the hidden treasures the "Accounting Operation" could not achieve.

Departure

Tuesday October 24, 1978, it was the day to set sail. I was driven to the river port Bến Gỗ of Biên Hòa with some of the Đặng family and I met Anna and Mary there. Besides the three of us, I was entrusted also with two teenagers, a third cousin Văn and the middleman's son named Nhiên.

It was quite a scene that morning for the sendoff. A handful of Public Security standing on the plank called out the names from the list that I compiled. Most of the passengers were sent below deck. My experiences with watercrafts were limited to paddleboat, rowboat or ferry, but the ship looked pretty scary to me, I could almost touch the water from the deck, I wondered whether this ship could sustain the big ocean waves.

Brother Ju-Xiang stood on shore among many people waved goodbye and wished us smooth sailing. It was an open farewell without any secrecy except the place was guarded and cordoned off.

Our ship was escorted by a patrol boat because we had to go through several jurisdictions. Reaching the open water, we stopped and were told that since we were leaving Vietnam for good so please leave our Vietnamese currency to the escorts; most people responded wholeheartedly and a bucketful of money was collected and handed over. The Public Security fired their AK-47s skywards then turned around.

Storm at Sea

Once reaching the sea—South China Sea of the Pacific Ocean, our ship began to rock gently and I started to throw up even was trying very hard to look to the horizon. I had heard about seasickness before and this round I knew what it meant to throw up the bile. My abdomen began spasmodic contraction that became so painful I almost fainted. If the baby came out during this time, I would not merely be helpless but a hindrance. Thank God that Anna did not get seasick at all, she was wondering that herself even years later.

By dusk, the wind and waves were growing in strength; our boat was tossed like a toy in the swells of an ocean that was anything but pacific. The captain belched out orders to the greenhorn deckhands in the bow to throw flip-flops into the water while he was at the stern to approximate the wavelengths of the ocean surface waves. I was horrified to see all the chaotic maneuvers on board and everyone was soaked with ocean sprays. The captain tried hard to steer the boat to go through the troughs and crests.

I was greatly alarmed when our ship tilted from side to side with the mast pointing more and more towards the horizon. After the third count of the violent move, a thought flashed in my mind that if the boat would flip one more time it must go belly up; miraculously, our boat turned upright again.

Now water was leaking through the cracks in the hull, all the deckhands rushed beneath deck to vacate the passengers and pump out the water with the Yanmar motors.

Finally, we had to return for repair.

In the morning, we were served a hot breakfast of rice soup which was the most horrible meal I had tasted ever. Instead of a heartwarming comfort to the empty stomachs, nobody could swallow one bit of it because Mr. Đặng's oldest daughter cooked it with sea water!

Return to Land

As our boat went into the estuary we witnessed a historical event in the making: the first chartered freighter of the boat people exodus. On a rusty ship high above us, on its deck sat a huge crowd sheltering from the sun under plastic sheets in different colors. We looked up as they were watching us from above, knowing full well that we all were the "open-exit" boat people. It was October 26.

(The junked freighter called Hai Hong—Rainbow of the Sea, brought 2,000-plus refugees to Hong Kong. It was not permitted to enter HK and anchored for months on the outer banks until the HK government and the UN High Commissioner for Refugees reached an agreement. These refugees were housed in cheap hotels in Kowloon and free to work in the booming plastic flower factories. Some families made thousands of dollars there. Boat people landed in HK later were not so lucky but kept in prisons; many stayed there for ten or more years and got repatriated to VN; some committed suicide in protest. Many people were rejected for resettlement due to the want of relationship to the former Government or ARVN. Many earlier refugees were lucky to resettle in the West even they could be categorized as refugees of nonpolitical causes. There were so many tragedies of the boat people and volumes had been written to chronicle their sufferings.)

We returned to Biên Hòa and stayed in a vacant warehouse, immediately Ju-Xiang came to see us. After paying our passage fees our family had three taels of gold on hand, so Anna went a local midwife to get some rest prior to the delivery. During that two-week stay Anna got many vitamin B12 shots and good meals.

While on land, we heard that the packed river barge which left port same day as ours was no more.

It's A Boy!

On early morning of Tuesday, October 31, a baby boy came! The news got back home, my Father who did not go see Mary after she was born in a hospital nearby, came with Mom in a Taxi to welcome their third grandson twenty miles away.

I did not have the opportunity to name our daughter when I was detained in Long-Khánh; this turn I named our son Hui-Quan. The middle name Hui (sunlight) joined to his sister's middle name Chun (spring) expressing motherly love as sunshine in spring. These two words became well-known through a poem "A Traveler's Ballad" by Meng Jiao of the Tang dynasty:

> Thread in loving mother's handling
> Hastens clothes for lad outgoing
> Tightly stitching prior to departing
> Dreadful of a tardy homecoming
> Well may tiny unworthy endearing
> Repay threesome sunshine of spring?

A fortnight later, we set out for the second time. Our family had a free passenger and the ship took on even more people. Like the previous time, a Public Security read out names from the roster and people boarded the boat. The sendoff was smaller because we only were leaving.

Kids once again were put below deck, but no sooner when my third cousin Văn rushed up and handed back in tears the baby to Anna because he turned blue due to the lack of air down under. Since a new born baby boy to the Chinese was a good omen, so Mr. Đặng allowed Anna, the baby and I sat on the bench in the cabin where we could see the back of the pilot. For some reason the original captain was dismissed and we had a new pilot, a Lt. J.G.

Trip Number Two

Reenacting the same script, the escorting boat asked for donation followed by a farewell salvo of AK-47s, and then we headed out to sea.

After an hour or so, the boat engine suddenly stalled and everyone was horrified. The mechanics worked frantically beneath in the engine room, finally after half an hour which seemed like a century, the engine restarted and everybody cheered. The engine had no more hiccup since then.

This turn there was not even one bit of sea breeze, the signal flags hung on the mast were motionless. I asked the pilot about the flags, he told me that they read "ship in distress, needs help." This round I had plenty of time to observe the South China Sea. The water was murky as black ink and frequently we encountered drifting leaves, twigs, papers, plastic bags, plastic pails and torn nets. The next day, a ship appeared to sail towards us, and many on our boat were excited wishing the ship might pick us up; soon it changed direction and vanished from sight. The captain said it was impossible to tell what that was; it could be a pirate ship.

Some listened to BBC and the news was not very encouraging: a newly set up refuge island in Malaysia was holding twenty thousand people with only four water wells; many boats had been intercepted by the Malaysian Navy, latched on with cables then dragged to the open ocean and capsized.

We had no other choices but keep going. Our captain steered our boat to the northern shore of Malaysia under the cover of darkness and in order to prevent from being pulled out by the Malaysian Navy he forced our boat onto a rocky beach at dawn. The plot worked, the bow of our boat was lodged firmly among big rocks.

Crash Landing—Malaysia

It was the morning of November 17 of 1978, we landed on the beach south of Terengganu (it was on that day hundreds of people belonged to the People's Temple cult killed themselves in Jonestown of Guyana). The sailors were ordered to destroy all the five-gallon plastic jugs; some broke the hull and let in water to disable the boat. From my experience in the past, so I got hold of a plastic jug which proved to be very useful later. During the chaos and exhilaration the sailors and young folks jumped in the chest-deep water helping passengers to wade ashore. The militias were on the beach; one sailor went to them and got his front tooth knocked off by a rifle butt!

Anna was peaceful and quiet during the entire trip, with unknown power she sat through the trip holding the baby without going to the toilet or lying down; now she became very nervous to leave the boat and leap into the water. A sailor helped her wading to the beach. I put our baby in the plastic baby bathtub and handed it to a young man. When we were on land, we ran around the heap of belongings to look for our baby. We found him in the tub under somebody's clothing; and there were sands on his face kicked up by the crowd running between the beach and the boat. In the chaos, our baby boy did not get crushed.

Immediately, a news reporter came. I was told by Mr. Đặng to tell him that our boat was overcrowded because after picking up passengers from a sinking boat so that the Malaysian authority would not suspect we came out "openly". Reluctantly, I followed Mr. Đặng's instruction even though I disagreed to his reasoning. It turned out to be futile as I thought, he was only a reporter and the soldiers could not make decision for us.

It was going to rain and we were allowed to move to a vacant mansion on the nearby hill. It was a wide open place that probably had been used to shelter other refugees.

In the afternoon, a group of young men from a nearby refugee camp of Kota Baru came. They carried bags of rice on their shoulders. The group leader, an ARVN Captain wanted to meet the representative of our boat and he demanded that the leader must be a former officer and able to speak English, so the role fell on me. The Captain told me that they had plenty of rice in their camp more than what they could consume so they shared the surplus with all the new arrivals. He told me quietly that I should keep one bag of rice for myself and distributed the rest; he knew that we officers not like the other refugees were dirt poor. That bag of rice played an important role in sustaining our family on the refugee island. What a practical guy!

Every family or related groups joined together and prepared their own meals. While Anna was preparing the rice soup, I killed a lizard on a nearby bush with a tree branch, someone roasted the lizard and the meat was added to the soup. Mary was so hungry that we had to prevent her from sucking in the steaming soup too fast.

By the advice from some seniors to urge people come together in following the Chinese proverb that once you have been on a boat then you are part of the big family. I stood up and spoke to the whole group to join hands and go to the nearby village to secure cooking utensils for a common kitchen. I spoke loudly for ten to fifteen minutes and asked for input; gradually I lost my voice and had to step down. People dispersed and ventured to the nearby village. That proverb did not work out but it proved another saying that people were selfish even after going through hardship together, you should only take care of yourself.

I was grumbling inside of what a cruel fate I had, just landed on a foreign soil after all these years of trouble and I got for trying to help each other out was the loss of my voice! An old lady realized that I got laryngitis and she offered a folk remedy. She gave me a lime to roast on open flame, scrape off the charred rind, crush the lime, pour on hot water, add a pinch of salt and drink it while warm. My voice returned to normal the next morning.

I strolled down to the beach, lo and behold more than half of the aft of our boat had been torn away by the incessant pounding waves. Strewn among the rocks were the rusty remains of several boat engines which might be the residues of other refugee ships.

Terengganu

In the late afternoon, we were led on to many buses with our belongings. After half an hour or so, we came to a wharf. Some Chinese folks walked around the buses and handed out breads, from them we knew that we were in Terengganu and heading to the infamous Pulau Bidong refugee island which we learned from the BBC news. Some people wrote brief letters and requested those good Samaritans to mail them to Vietnam.

Camp Pulau Bidong

We were transported to the island on a big boat and no one needed to stay under deck this time. The trip took more than an hour and we arrived at Pulau Bidong at dusk. There were so many people on shore to watch the newcomers and I was seen by my eldest brother Ju-Hua who left Vietnam on a different boat and came there a few days ahead of us. (Pulau Bidong refugee camp opened on August 8, 1978 and closed on November 11, 1991.)

We hunkered down in front of a simplistic wooden structure and a guy read out a brief welcome message and regulations of the refugee camp. The appointed Camp Representative was Đỗ Cao Minh DDS, brother of the late General Đỗ Cao Trí.

After that the process of registration began and our boat was assigned a number for resettlement interview and food distribution, either event would be announced through the P.A. system. Immediately I handed in our approved immigration papers hoping that we would go to America very soon.

The first matter next morning was looking for a place to stay. Somehow we joined a family whose head was a distant relative of Mom and his wife was the old lady who gave me the lime which restored my voice. They bought a place in the uphill section of the island for 200 dollars. The place consisted of a skeleton of crooked trees with a bunk made out of salvaged planks as the centerpiece. All I had carried in my wallet was a twenty-dollar bill, I handed them over to contribute towards the purchase price for one of the two blue tarpaulins served as covering. Since our baby boy was recognized having brought good luck to the boat, and newborn baby and nursing mother must not sleep on the ground so Anna and the baby shared the bed with two other women in that family in spite of our miniscule partnership of the shed.

Anna was upset all these years that I did not bring more dollars when leaving Vietnam. My idea was that once landed on a free country we should be able to get some money from America. The dollars remained back home would help my parents to hang on till they immigrate legally to the States, and who could tell we survive the voyage or not bump into pirates? In retrospect, we were able to get around insurmountable difficulties time and again but by the goodness and mercy from the Lord.

Not that far from our shed, further up the hill, I bumped into Cousin Chen Shao-Ji, son of our First Uncle, with his wife and four children. They came out for free for he piloted a boat! I remembered vaguely he told us that he had been a seafarer, but as a pilot I was not that sure. Anyway, he made it.

I volunteered as interpreter in the camp so that I could help both Chinese and Vietnamese in their interviews by the U.S. Delegation. One day, a young Vietnamese couple with a child came for interview and the interviewer asked for the husband's military qualifications. The man showed his paper that he was in the Popular Force during the war. By resettlement standard Popular Force was quasi-military and was categorized even below the Police Force, therefore his application was rejected point blank; nevertheless, he could apply to resettle in other countries. This young man asked me to beg the interviewer to reconsider his case, I told him that it was no use because he failed to meet the requirement and I had no saying whatsoever in this matter. Some days later, I met this man near our shed and he gave me a very obnoxious look. I was not scared of what he could do to me there, but as an idiom in all three languages of Chinese, English, and Vietnamese: no good deed goes unpunished.

For us, we would resettle in the States, not because of I had served in the ARVN but because our immigration had been approved before we left Vietnam. Per my knowledge in the camp, any one had served in the military would most likely be welcomed to the States. Some families fled the country without husbands or fathers; if the family members could provide the ARVN serial numbers then they would resettle in the States.

After establishing correspondence with my brother Ju-Jiang in Maryland, we received several parcels with baby clothing and medicines. My brother did send us some money but they never arrived.

During our four months on the refugee island food supply to the camp was skimpy. We received rice ten times one pound per capita, dried fish two or three times, and beef once. Thank God that I had kept the twenty-five-pound bag of rice from the Kota Baru refugees that we were not starved to death.

As a nursing mother needed much more than mere rice, Anna had to sell off all the wedding jewelry from Mom, majority of the contents of the parcels from America, sold also was the Seiko-5 watch that I was keeping as memorabilia of my deceased brother. We asked my cousin's wife to handle the selling of all our stuffs and buying our foods in the beachfront open air market. The baby aspirins from the U.S. were sold fifty cents each.

I tried to start an English class as others did but I did not get any student willing to pay. I quit after teaching a few classes for free, I needed to conserve my energy.

In comparison, food supply on the island was worse than the rice rations in the "reeducation" camps I went through, though they were small in quantity yet constant. The water issue was relieved until freighters brought water from the mainland, not to say the constant worry for fire hazard due to the disorderly and overcrowded dwellings. I tried desperately to leave the island as soon as possible. I confided my worries to Anna that we would agree to go to any country that would host us.

An opportunity came when BBC was to recruit a few workers. I registered and took a written test along with hundreds of people. One morning the test result was announced over the P.A. system and I was one of the seven who had passed the test. Everyone in the shed congratulated us assuming soon we would leave the island ... but nothing happened.

A woman from our boat left the island after only a month and half, but we had no such luck.

One day people swarmed to the beach to have a glimpse of a visitor from the States. He must be quite influential to have arranged the boat trip coming to see his family through the authority of the U.N., Malaysia, and the American Embassy. The Ông family was very rich and well-known in the Chinese community in Vietnam; I was certain that they got immigration approval from the U.S. but had to take the treacherous route of fleeing by sea.

One morning I was volunteering in the camp office, Nhiên rushed in telling me to go home at once that our baby was on the brink of death. I ran back to the shed and he was just revived. What happened was that while Anna bathed the baby in the wide-open shed, he was choked with mucus and turned blue. Anna cried for help and the old lady in the shed quickly rubbed medicated oil on the chest and the back of our boy, then he pissed and began to cry, and his complexion returned to normal. The good luck baby did not become the second casualty of VT333 buried on the island after the death of a senior gentleman.

One day my brother's sister-in-law Suong and her children came to the front of our shed and yelled that Anna was selling the diamonds stolen from her, because the person bought the diamonds described Anna's unique facial features. Although she had never met Anna, but knew that it was Anna. I yelled back at her and they left.

Anna had never been so tarnished by such a lie. Suong, of course, had met Anna during Anna's three-year stay with my parents. The tale that Suong had lost a paper bag filled with diamonds had had caused havoc in our home. Suong claimed that when her home was searched during the Accounting Operation, she came and handed her sister, i.e. my sister-in-law, a bunch of diamonds in a paper bag. My sister-in-law in a hurry allegedly did not know what were inside, and left the bag somewhere downstairs. When my sister-in-law came to realize that diamonds were in the bag but it was gone. At first the maid of the family that renting our first floor was blamed for taking the bag, after the baseless accusation was rejected my sister-in-law shifted the blame to Anna. My parents of course did not believe the illogical tale. Later on, my sister-in-law instructed her three children to chorus whenever they encountered Anna at home: Picking up diamonds, got TB (which was a curse). And now Anna was accused of selling diamonds on the island!

This staged drama out of the blue not only Anna was maliciously slandered but also extremely embarrassed, for right after those troublemakers departed, the old lady told her family in Cantonese, not knowing that Anna could understand them "Watch your purse!"

Prior to 1975 Suong had gathered a small fortune by utilizing her husband's position as a powerful Police officer through black market deals. Her husband Lê văn Đức was one of those silly guys that had left Vietnam in the last minute decided to return to Vietnam after arriving at Guam. They returned on the ship Việt Nam Thương Tín, namely the Commercial Trust of Vietnam. All the returnees were sent directly to "reeducation". Ten plus years went by, Đức was released from the camp and came to the States through the Orderly Departure Program of the U.N. Đức tried to reunite with the family but was rejected by his wife because he became a nobody. Sương opened a carryout and put her children to work instead of attending college. Sương forced her oldest daughter to marry a Chinese for money, later on the daughter became a mental case by the abusive spouse. Poor girl! Per Anna that girl was very gentle and polite.

Eventually Sương exhibited her true self. She and her youngest brother came to visit Washington D.C., they stayed overnight in our parents' apartment. The next morning she told Mom that several thousand dollars had disappeared from her purse. In a fury, my parents kicked them out and had nothing to do with her ever since.

One day I met Mr. Yee who lent us the gold, he noticed my long and unkempt hairs, and he gave me one Malaysian dollar to have a haircut.

Camp Kuala Lumpur

On March 23, 1979 the six of us left the refugee island went to Kuala Lumpur and stayed in the transit camp located on the property of the Sungei Besi Catholic Church. There were long rows of wooden lattices on which we spent the day and slept at night. Food was no more in short supply here, three meals a day plus plenty of instant noodles for those volunteered to serve meals. In the morning, I worked with a group to boil water for the condensed milk in electric boilers that were six feet tall.

There were hundreds of people staying in this temporary shelter, getting water was time-consuming from a few trickling faucets.

Mary got scabies in her ear canal. It took several weeks of medication to get rid of the problem after we came to America.

Most people stayed in the transit camp only for a couple weeks, but we had to go through immigration red tapes and stayed there for two months. During that period we went to the Embassy for portraits and fingerprinting. In that unique trip to the Embassy we took for the first time a high-speed elevator going up to the thirtieth floor, I could feel the blood rushing to my head. It was the only opportunity we passed through a commercial district in Kuala Lumpur, the fragrance from the stores there gave me a very special impression.

In the transit camp, I heard for the first time the term autism. An autistic six year old boy, sitting on the lattice bed and played something put down by his father, all day long by himself.

There I met two high school classmates and Dr. Trần Thanh Sơn from the Pleiku Military Hospital, he was the first Vietnamese Protestant I knew.

International Collect Call

I heard that in the church office we could make collect calls to the States. So I called to my brother Ju-Jiang in Maryland, there were so much to talk about; the phone call might have lasted for an hour. When I enquired about it later, my brother would not reveal how much was that international collect call, but smiled.

Luggage-Free Travelers

Many people in the transit camp sneaked out to Kuala Lumpur to buy suits, dresses and boom boxes. We had spent the little sum of money from selling everything for food on the island; therefore we could not afford even the taxi fare going out. Our short-term neighbors also from VT333 were nice to us; a woman altered some used adult clothing to make a dress for Mary. My classmate Thái văn Hùng found out that all I had for footwear were the free flip-flops; he gave me twenty dollars for a pair of sneakers from a trader at the church's gate.

Chapter 6.

New Continent and New Life in Christ

It was May 23, 1979, exactly four years of going home after skipping POW camp. What a morning it was! After tossing and turning on the lattice bed the whole night, we had our regular breakfast of sandwich bread and condensed milk, then boarded a bus in front of the Church with our simple belongings. We waved goodbye to Văn, Nhiên and the crowd behind the gate

In the air terminal, refugee passengers with Malaysian currency got in line to exchange them to dollars and I was not one of them. All the check-in procedure and boarding passes were handled by the UNHCR personnel. All we had for the family of four fit comfortably in an Australian Army knapsack that my family gave me in the last "reeducation" camp visit. Each family carried a large white plastic bag emblazoned with blue letters of ICEM—Council of the Intergovernmental Committee for European Migration containing travel documents and chest X-rays.

One More Glance of Vietnam

On a Malaysian Airline DC-10, we sat among a large group of retiree tourists from the States in colorful Hawaiian shirts. An hour later, voice of the pilot from the P.A. directed our attention to look down to our left the coastline of Vietnam. The distance took our boat chucking at five knots per hour for three days and two nights was only an hour's flight in a jetliner. I sent my heart to the land that I loved but could not return, I did not know whom to thank for in all the mysterious twists and turns of our lives; and now we embarked on a new leg of life's journey ...

Hong Kong Layover

We landed in Hong Kong Kai Tak Airport and were transported to a hotel in Kowloon. That was a hotel occupied by refugees waited for resettlement to the free world; they were more fortunate than those of us in the refugee camps in Southeast Asia. Although they were clamped in the small rooms of the dilapidated hotel but the situation was better than many people in Saigon before 1975. They had in-house toilets, running water and stoves, all for free and they could go out to earn money or sightsee at leisure. We were treated dinner on the sixth floor terrace. It was more than six months for us to have a meal of bok choy stir-fried with pork and some soup. After dinner Kiệt, brother of Ms. Đào Quỳnh, an new acquaintance in the Sungei Besi camp, came to pick us up and took us for a quick tour of the Pearl of the Orient. For some reason, I was impressed by a store where there were springs of all kinds and all sizes in containers, on the floor, or hanging from the ceiling. Kiệt invited us to a café but I declined to order any food or drink because I had stuffed myself in the hotel. It was getting dark and when the three of us, two men and Mary, waiting for the signal at a crosswalk, I looked but did not see Anna and the baby. Hurriedly we turned around and finally located them after a couple minutes;

Anna must had been dazzled by the store window display and got separated from us by the fast-paced Hong Kong crowd. From then on we escorted her every step of the way.

With Kiệt's recommendation I bought a digital Seiko watch costing 400 HK dollars, approximately eighty U.S. dollars. If I realized the value of dollars by then I would not have purchased such a fancy watch. Kiệt also led us to ride the double-decked bus going through the newly completed tunnel under the Hong Kong Strait. Before Kiệt left, he handed us a luggage containing twenty pieces of silk cloths to be picked up by his relative in Virginia and we were given one piece of material as our compensation. Kiệt entertained us with a sightseeing tour for a courier service of 2,000-dollar worth of merchandise from the East to the West; we were entrusted with such a task probably because Đào Quỳnh had paid close attention on us in the transit camp. (Later on, we paid Quỳnh 200 dollars for the watch plus another piece of silk we gifted to our hostess.)

Next morning, we boarded a Pan Am Boeing 747 bound for Tokyo. The noticeable differences were not only in the interior of the aircraft compared to that of the DC-10 and the meals but also the costume and the age of the stewardesses. The Malaysians were young, lively in their colorful sarongs; the older Pan Am crews wore drab uniforms and were disinterested.

After a few hours of layover in Tokyo Narita Airport, we boarded another Pan Am Jumbo Jet, which was new. The pilot greeted the passengers through the P.A. system and informed us that this new version of Jumbo jet was to fly over the North Pole with a shorter fuselage and carried more fuels. How exciting it was for those who had never been in a jet and now skipping continents in the modern means of air travel in two consecutive days. These jet travels were so luxurious in comparison to what I had in the civilian DC-3, DC-4, DC-6, the military C-7, C-119, C-130 and Huey helicopter; they gave me from the hurting eardrums to a convulsing stomach when the plane dropped hundreds of feet in tropical thunderstorm. The pilot announced when we were atop the Arctic Circle that our Jumbo jet was traveling at 700 mph with prevailing tailwind. After fourteen hours we landed on Kennedy Airport.

New York, New York

It was Saturday March 24, 1979 we arrived at America, our new homeland!

A short while before landing, all passengers were handed immigration papers to fill in, I put down the contact information with my brother's address in Columbia, Maryland. In the airport we were rushed through the customs by a female refugee worker while the other refugees were photographed and fingerprinted.

In a hotel adjacent to the airport, our family and my eldest brother's family, four adults and five children were put into a room with four double beds. The refugees were served a two-course meal in the hotel dining room. Everyone was excited, I was wondering why we were flown to NYC instead of Washington DC. In the hotel lobby I bought a bag of disposable shavers for three dollars. Later on when I described my purchase to one of our sponsors in Connecticut, who happened to be a Gillette razor salesman, he exclaimed that it was an outright robbery. Welcome to New York City!

Hartford, Connecticut

Next day our two families were bused to the La Guardia to wait for a flight to… Hartford. Why? I scratched my head.

We were hungry with no breakfast, it was cold in May that year and we just came from the tropics without any warm clothing. A lady refugee worker gave me a bill of twenty to buy breakfast from the Airport cafeteria. I roamed around the place and took a peek of the food under the sneeze guards and the price started from three dollars. Because I did not know what to buy therefore ended up with nothing. After waiting for an hour or so, we were told that there was problem to arrange flying to Hartford so we would go by limousine instead.

Before noon, we arrived in Hartford and went to a United States Catholic Conference office. We were welcomed by Don Charron, a retired Sgt. Maj. who had served in Vietnam. It turned out that we were sent to Hartford due to a last-minute change of mind from our brother. When Ju-Jiang realized that he could not afford to house nine members from two families plus two teenagers that accompanied me, in turn USCC took over without hesitation. Anna was comfortable with this unexpected arrangement from her community of faith, as for me it was a good time to meet the people from the religion that I was interested to take up.

Pretty soon, two men from the sponsoring church—St. Pius X Roman Catholic Church in Middletown came to pick us up. We were riding in the Cougar of George Trowbridge and Ju-Hua's family was put in the station wagon of Jim DeLude.

Middletown, Connecticut

We were driven to Middletown and staying with the Vela's. Our hosts Al and Carlene Vela had three children Bert, Marty and Julie (Juliana); they moved recently from Anaheim, California to the East Coast to be close to Carlene's family. Al got his job as ESOL director in a school system in Connecticut. Their house had once been owned by the mayor, a Cape Cod in an upper class neighborhood with swimming pools. We stayed in a small but cozy room across from the owners'. To adjust to the twelve-hour time zone difference between Southeast Asia and the East Coast of the United States, we slept in and out in the first week.

Gradually, people of the refugee reception committee from the Church came to see us. Besides our host the Velas, there were my brother Ju-Hua's hosts Jim and Marge DeLude, Emil and Jane Lavigne, Frank and Esther Quintana, Bob and

New Continent and New Life in Christ

Muriel Sweeney, Frank and Eileen Hilsdon, Tom and Ann Goodin, George and Rachel Trowbridge. After we moved to our townhouse they came to help in grocery shopping, medical and dental care, and English lessons for Anna, driving practice for me.

The next day, we contacted Ju-Jiang. On the following weekend he and his wife drove up to Connecticut and on the way picked up our mutual friend, Hoksee Lee, from New York City.

It was an exciting reunion and we chatted for a long time at the meal table. It was during one of those meals that USCC called to inform me that the two teenagers accompanied me had arrived and the Vietnamese nun on the phone waited for my agreement to receive them. My brother and sister-in-law recommended that we should let them stay with USCC for they would be better taken care of while we had yet settled down. It sounded very reasonable to me, so I told the nun that we were unable to take them in. The nun became furious and threatened me that it would be impossible for me to contact or to see them from then on. I did not know that my decision resulted in regrettable situations for the two teenagers; neither would I know what happen if I took the recommendation from the Velas to take the teens under our wings.

A few days later, we attended our first ever Memorial Day parade on Main Street of Middletown. When the lone Yankee soldier was walking home, I explained the concluding scene to Anna, deep down I was touched. The Vietnam War had nothing to do with slavery but lasted for more than thirty years. We emigrated to the West through unbeknownst arrangement while many people who had brushed shoulders with us vanished. All the human conflicts brought tremendous loss of lives and severe hardship especially on the losing side.

Almost like vacationing in our new hometown, we were shown the ways of daily life, and introduced to the grocery, department stores, bank, etc. There in 1979, I tried my hand to use an ATM machine in a bank in Middletown when it was first promoted. I remembered Bell's telephone was also experimented successfully in Connecticut. Thanks to the educational opportunity I had back home, our hostess Carlene commented that I was like a neighbor across the street had had no problem in communication and learned all the new things with ease. Before we moved out, she told me that we could ask for anything from her kitchen except the microwave oven which was a new gadget at the time.

I got a free hair cut from the neighborhood barber and dental care for both of us from their dentist whom we referred to as the "Chicken Dentist" for he looked like Purdue the chicken guy. The dentist took out my third molar with a huge cavity that might have caused me severe trouble in the refugee camps. I learned to use the riding lawn mower and rake the grass and leaves. We enjoyed the piano demonstration from Juliana from a baby grand with her favorite piece "The Vagabond."

After a week or so we received our Permanent Resident cards or Green Cards in the mail, and then we went to Hartford to apply for Social Security numbers. Many refugees got their Green Cards after one or two years. Our situation was uncommon, for we came as boat people but were not categorized as refugees, therefore we could not get housing assistance, financial assistance, free education, or job training. The free gift we got was the airfare. Refugees were required to pay back their airfares in installments beginning six months after their arrivals.

Through the efforts of the Church, a few weeks later we moved to a rental townhouse community a mile or so from our host family. All things considered, it was truly our first home.

Job Interviews

Even before our move, the Church was busy hunting jobs for me. The first interview I went to was Raymond Machined

Products, a factory with vast open space and some workers were making rubber products like fan belts. The interviewer knew about my past experience and when strolling near an eye-washing station he mentioned casually that if I could administer first aid in case of workplace emergency. I declined the job because of the gasoline fumes in there. Then I was informed about a job opening at Olin Skis to polish skis with ten percent extra pay for the graveyard shift. Although I was badly in need of a job but I had never been a night owl hence it was out of the question.

Machine Shop

Eventually I was given a job with Ajax Screw Machines in the town of Berlin, approximately fifteen miles away. George Denison from the Church linked me up with the shop owned by his mother-in-law and he was a foreman there. George had to drive me to work until I purchased a car, after that we went to work in carpool.

The factory had about twelve employees; half a dozen or so men working on the big machines that cut hexagonal steel rods into nuts, and I was on the next link to cut threads on the blank nuts using four thread millers.

The threading operation took about forty seconds and I milled around among the four machines mounting on the blank nuts and dismounting the threaded ones. This incessant motion could quickly exhaust and frustrate the operator and it might be the reason I got the job; if not for the camps I had gone through and my "young" age of early thirties, I doubted I could keep the job for long.

During the operation I used a gauge to test the threads on the finished nuts, when the threads were tight or loose to the touch I informed my foreman Ed Sutherland to see if the cutter needed to be sharpened or replaced. The milling operation used heavy-grade cutting oil and pretty soon my clothes and sneakers from Malaysia were spattered with oil.

There were two to three ladies, each one of them worked on a miller of different type that used water-based green-colored cutting fluids.

The shop was very noisy because of the big machines and I had not thought of protecting my hearing, for no one used earmuffs. When the office phone rang, it triggered a flashing red light on the factory wall as well as very loud beeps to overcome the noise.

My starting pay was five dollars an hour. My first paycheck of three days' work was more than twice that of my monthly pay in the ARVN.

In imitating other coworkers' example, I bought breakfast from a food truck, but pretty soon began to bring my own meals. I bought a lunch box with thermos and packed my sandwiches, fruit, and V8 or tomato juice. Even though I used to salty foodstuff but not for long I had to give up my canned vegetable juices.

The factory had overtime work all the time and no one ever complained. A guy from Germany came to work with an alcoholic breath. An African American was Puerto Rican.

Pig Feet Soup

Standing nine to ten hours a day at work my shins started to ache and my feet were swelling. I remembered the tale of pig feet, why not try some? So we went to the supermarket which did carry them and Anna cooked the soup with mixed vegetables. Voila! The swelling went away and the aching shinbones bothered me no more. This experience reversed my poor view on folk medicine but instead appreciated its therapeutic effectiveness on some common ailments.

My eldest brother Ju-Hua worked in a factory in the neighboring town of Portland that manufactured jet engine blades. His job also required standing long hours and started to experience pain in his shins, so he tried the pig feet soup which also worked for him. From then on he ate pig feet once every week to keep his own in shape.

First Loan

Through my brother Ju-Jiang, our pen pal David Smith generously agreed to lend me $5,000 from his Postal Service Federal Credit Union under a three-year term with the same interest rate that the FCU was paying him. What a friend!

In the summer, the machine shop shutdown for two weeks and everybody had time off with pay. Since I was new I got only a week's pay, the other week I could earn money by cleaning up the factory's lightings. In the first week, we took the Greyhound Bus to Maryland to meet our newly arrived parents. It was the first time I realized somewhat the "danger" of New York when we stopped by the Port Authority bus terminal. Even inside the men's restroom, two security guards were standing to keep watch, and all the policemen patrolling inside were in pairs.

First Gospel Encounter

On the bus, we were busy with a four year old girl and a nine month old boy, a middle-aged Oriental man carrying a small Bible approached me to share the "Gospel." He was a Chinese pastor from Burma. Arrogantly I replied that I needed not that kind of stuff for I was a Catholic. He went back to his seat and read his Bible.

Community College

Planning to get a college degree for a better career and if possible to finish my pharmacy education, I registered at Middlesex Community College taking two courses of English and Biology. Bob Sweeney drove me to the first evening class. The teacher of English was very talkative, with a blushing face I guessed from much drinking at dinner; he mumbled through the hour and I could not even make out one bit out of his monologue.

Bell's Palsy

A few days later, one weekday evening of September, I went home in George's truck, since it was quite warm inside the car, I lowered the window for some fresh air. September in Connecticut was cold and when I realized the wind rushing against my right ear was too cold I cranked up the window. After a shower at home and went grocery shopping with Anna I began to feel pain in my ear and it was getting worse by and by, so after dinner I took a painkiller and went to bed.

Around midnight I woke up and felt better. I went to the bathroom, turned on the light and saw a different me in the mirror. My right face did not belong to me, it had been paralyzed. I could not shut my right eye or talk normally. In my heart I was cursing the fate I had, spending all those bitter years and now only a few months in this new country and I was in another big mess? I woke Anna up and she called up our brother in Maryland and in turn he called up the Velas, they came when it was in the wee hours and brought me to the Middlesex Memorial Hospital. The Emergency Room physician checked me out and advised me to seek help elsewhere in the morning.

Facial Nerve Decompression

Finally, for some reason, I decided (hastily as usual) to choose surgery to take care of the palsy. I had a mastoidectomy and facial nerve decompression by an otolaryngologist Dr. Keat-Jin Lee in the St. Raphael Hospital in New Haven. His basis for the surgery was that Bell's palsy was caused by the swelling of the facial nerve, or cranial nerve number seven, it was the only nerve in the body that was housed in a bony sheath and when the swelling of the nerve did not go away could lead to its death; decompression was the removal of the bony sheath so that the nerve could expand freely and recover after the swelling went away. After the surgery my facial control got back to about sixty percent but I could whistle no more. In an audiology test, the physician confirmed my loss of hearing in the higher pitch.

Since the onset of Bell's palsy I could not attend classes and Mr. Sweeney helped me to get the refund of tuition. That was the only official college education I got in the States.

While I was recuperating at home, I witnessed my first snowfall on October 10, 1979.

In the follow up visit Dr. Lee told me that I had the thickest skull that he ever encountered, it took him more than an hour to open it up using an electric drill.

My sickness occurred right after the three-month probation period, all the medical expenses were covered by my employer's insurance, except I had to pay twenty percent of the surgeon's bill. I got a bill from Dr. Lee of $400, the sum of money I did not have, so I tried my luck by sending him a note telling him about having been a refugee in Malaysia (Dr. Lee's home country) and a new comer to the States. Hope against hope, even though I had had bad luck all these times, around Christmas time I received a cancelled bill from his office, the $400 crossed out and written on top of it: "Courtesy from Dr. Lee." How happy I was, there were good people on earth!

Driver License

I had driven Jeeps for more than four years followed by a period of inactivity for four years, so George Trowbridge took me to reacquaint with the road in his Opel, a small car with automatic shift. Before the driving test, I took the written and driving test once and passed, when handing me the paperwork for the license, the examiner reminded me that I should go over my driver's manual, because I only met the minimum requirement of fifteen correct answers out of twenty questions.

First Car

My first car was a 1970 American Motor Company Rebel four-door sedan on November 17. The purchase price was $550, with seven percent sales tax, eleven dollars registration fee, five dollars title fee, it came to $604.50. The used car dealer was in New Haven, an acquaintance of George Trowbridge. It was a three-speed stick shift with a straight six engine; a very powerful car even when I mistakenly started to move at third gear, it made no difference at all. The speedometer cable had broken therefore speed was a guesswork. On the way driving my first ever "owned" car to his home, George let me go first. Arriving at the destination, George told me that he was so concerned that I would get a speeding ticket because I was going at eighty five mph! His two daughters helped to wash and clean our "new" ten-year-old car.

Church Friends and Neighbors

Our family got a lot of help from the people from the Church as well as from some new friends. Anna got English lessons from Mrs. Esther Elphick, a Protestant Filipina, her husband was teaching history at Yale; a Vietnamese couple Mr. and Mrs. Nghi Lê. A Cantonese lady, Mrs. Loh who lived in the townhouse community, was a retired movie star from Hong Kong, frequented our home to befriend with Anna. There were no Vietnamese restaurants in the vicinity, so the Lohs wanted to try out the one in Hartford. I went with them in their Trans Am Firebird. The egg rolls there was so unauthentic I had to apologize to the Lohs that egg rolls were not supposed to be shaped as triangular wedges.

After the probation I got a raise to five fifty. At Thanksgiving I got my first turkey, which gave Anna a hard time to prepare. At Christmas I got a bonus check of $250 to buy a nineteen-inch Philco color television set and we returned the small B&W TV to Frank and Eileen.

I got another promotion to six dollars after New Year. One day my foreman Ed casually asked me how much I was making, unsuspiciously I responded. A few days later, on the way home, George said that I had done a big no-no; it almost caused a riot in the shop, because one of the ladies was making four fifty an hour after ten years. From then on my first friendly advice to a newcomer to the States was not to reveal personal salary to anyone. Objectively speaking, I did not ask for a raise, it was the kindness from the owner; next I was paid higher because I worked harder in operating four machines simultaneously, my production was timed with a stopwatch by Ed the foreman, and I attained an average productivity of eighty five percent. One day I was transferred to operate a big machine that cut the steel rods into blank nuts, less than an hour into the process I was pulled back to my old job because the four machines were too much for my replacement.

Sacraments

I informed the Church of my desire to join the Catholic Community. Without any religious classes or instructions, on the afternoon of Easter 1980, in a small chapel in the church I went through several Sacraments: Baptism, Confirmation, First Mass (no Confession), and Holy Matrimony. Finally we were husband and wife with the priest's blessings, Mary and William also received their baptism sacraments,

Job Change

After the sudden downturn of my facial nerve, my brother Ju-Jiang told me to come down to Maryland to stay away from the factory environment, not only I was developing skin rashes due to the cutting oil but also the 102 decibel noise was bad for my ears. During the two-week factory shutdown we visited Maryland and I went to an interview at a consulting firm and was hired.

Moving to Maryland

The Church group held a farewell party for us, with safety reminder driving with a trailer on the highway required a longer distance to brake. With a Jartran trailer filled with furniture on tow, we moved down to Rockville, Maryland in August 1980. We stayed with Ju-Xiang's family for two months then moved to our own apartment in the same community.

Financial Shock

My first paycheck was like a lightning bolt, my salary had lowered from six dollars to five, added also were state income tax and medical insurance premium that I did not have to worry about in my old job.

Now I lived only a hundred yard away from work and no need to pack lunches, the only expenditure I could trim was gasoline but car insurance still went up. My paycheck was barely able to cover our two-bedroom apartment's rent of $460 plus utility. The first thing I knew was to look for government assistance, so I applied for food stamps; we got approved for forty dollars a month, barely enough to feed a pet.

I was mad. Then I realized the reason why the Elphicks did not accept the teaching job at Georgetown University, it was expensive to live in the Washington D.C. metropolis. It was impossible and made no sense to turn back, so I had to look for additional incomes.

Desk Job

My job at the consulting firm was for the U.S. Environmental Protection Agency's Pre-Manufacture Notification or PMN in brief. Our deliverables were on a twenty-four-hour quick-turnaround basis. Our group of five people was to gather information of chemicals that were submitted to the EPA before put into production. Once getting an assignment, we would go through a set of pre-established references to list out all the available information on synonyms, chemical structure, acute and chronic toxicity, carcinogenicity, mutagenicity, teratogenicity and so forth, after that we looked up information online. By then personal computer was not available yet, we went online to access databases from the National Library of Medicine, and Lockheed Information which now called ProQuest. We used teletype-type machine linking up the online systems by a rubber-cupped handset through audio signals. The machine typed query commands and output data on the green-and-white papers.

Quite often we had to run two machines at the same time. On one occasion I ran all four machines simultaneously due to heavy workload, I accommodated the stressful demand and had no problems at all through my past experience in the machine shop. I saw a younger coworker who was in tears trying to run only two machines.

Daily we had to go to different libraries in the metropolitan region to duplicate paper copies from journals and books. We went to the National Library of Medicine in Bethesda, the largest of its kind in the world; the National Library of Agriculture in Beltsville, where microfilm printers produced photocopies still wet from the developing fluid.

Part-Time Job

Dad suffered many years from the multitudinous stones in one kidney, his family doctor Dr. Tseng recommended to have the bad kidney removed. The kidney got taken out was twice as big as the normal one.

When visiting our Father in Holy Cross Hospital after his surgery I saw the "wanted" ads posted besides the elevators for weekend dietary aides.

The hospital kitchen needed a lot of on-call workers and I was hired. After a couple weekends of on-the-job training then I should go to work only when called. Since I needed the money, so for a few weekends in a row I just showed up and punched in without waiting for the phone call, until one day I was told that I had to leave.

Seventy-Hour Workweek
Providentially, not much later a scheduled vacancy came up and I got the thirty hours per week job. It was sixteen hours on the weekend plus three evenings. There was some conflict of work schedule during those weekdays, with the sympathy from the project manager and the supervisor; I was Okayed to leave earlier to go to the second job.

At the kitchen of Holy Cross Hospital, I had worked in most stations there: tray line, dishwasher, pushed tray carts, prepared milkshake, wrapped snacks, washed pots and pans, mopped kitchen floor and dumped trash. Many of the returned trays from patients with unopened packets of cracker, fruit juice, milk cartons, apples, oranges etc. were trashed due to sanitation regulations; trays of hard-boiled eggs, roasted chickens, and pork chops were sent to the disposal or trash can.

In order to earn as much money as possible, twelve hours shifts were normal when I was needed, holidays with double pay were especially welcomed.

Tough Babysitting Money
Once, Anna tried to earn additional income from babysitting, so I went around the apartment complex taped up the tiny ads by the mail boxes advertising babysit service and we asked only a dollar an hour. Immediately we got a response to take care of a boy. After a full week of service it took me a couple trips to our client's apartment and was only successful in collecting the forty dollars fee after meeting the

boy's father. Some coworkers learned of Anna's service sent her their babies but only for a few hours each day.

Mental Breakdown

After several months of loneliness with two young children during the day seven days a week, Anna was far from home without close relatives nor friends and still adjusting to the new world, she became depressed. In Connecticut I worked normal hours and there were friends from the Church and English lessons from Mrs. Elphick; in here although my parents and brother were close by but could not help much. Anna hallucinated and heard voices; she saw the children as abominable puppies and wanted to kill them all. After the surfacing of her mental status, I brought her to see a Vietnamese psychiatrist in Arlington, Virginia. Dr. Trần Minh Tùng was a former Minister of Health. The diagnosis was swift; he gave Anna an injection and prescribed the classic anti-psychotic tricyclics. The medication put Anna to bed most of the time and brought along many side effects.

I had to quit my part-time job to take care of the family. By the compassionate sympathy from my supervisor and co-workers, I was able to take off as needed for laundry, doctor's visits, etc. Due to the loss of supplemental income, I requested a postponement of the $5,000 loan payment and was granted graciously by David our pen pal. I resumed the loan payment later and paid it off several months ahead of the schedule. How did we go through the crisis if not by the Lord's sustaining grace?

Trip to the Midwest

On the way to full recovery, Anna wanted to see her aunt and the families of two cousins lived in the suburb of Fort Smith, Arkansas. A cousin of Anna left Vietnam with her family at the verge of the Fall of Saigon in 1975. The other cousin fled Vietnam by boat with her four children, three girls and a boy in 1978. Her boat was ravaged by Thai pirates, the youngest daughter and the only boy died at sea and buried on a beach in Thailand, like many other deceased boat people, without coffins or tomb markings.

In order to prepare such a long trip, I brought the car to a transmission franchise which gave me an exorbitant quote exceeded the purchase price of our car. After learning about our needs, a coworker recommended her neighborhood transmission shop. The shop owner tested our car and assured me that it could handle the trip; he would take care of the car afterwards. So I drove halfway across the Continent also stopped by my cousins in Dallas, Texas without a glitch. After the promised maintenance from the auto shop our car stayed on the road for an additional five more years.

Put Anna to Work

After Anna's complete recovery, I had to take the psychiatrist's advice by putting Anna to work so that she could get away from the house and the children at least part of the day. So Anna worked part-time or temporarily at different jobs from grocery store, 7-Eleven, hotel, and department store, until she landed a job at the Dietary Department of Holy Cross Hospital after I quit the weekend position there.

The Catholic Church knew about the recovery of Anna from the prevalent depression among the expatriate Vietnamese; a deacon recommended that we would keep a statue of the Virgin Mary for a month to bless our home. When the small church group brought in the white gypsum statue and asked us to kneel down and recite Ava Maria. Somehow I felt that it was not right because it brought me the very unease I experienced in kneeling before idols when I was young.

Church-Organized Bible Study

It was 1984, the Vietnamese Catholic Church in Silver Spring promoted Bible reading in the congregation. The priest promulgated that the Papal Bull of John Paul II encouraged the Catholics to read the Bible and could even study the Word of God with the Protestants although they have strayed from the Faith, by doing so we could bring them back to see the True Light.

The priest started a Bible class in Saint Martin's Church in Gaithersburg. As a zealous Faithful new to the Roman Catholic Faith and it was a rare opportunity having the pastoring priest to lead the class. In the first evening of the class, besides the two of us, there were a few others. In the small study there was a pious and soft-spoken Chinese young man in black robe would soon enter a seminary in Taiwan. The priest started the study by telling us that he just got some exciting news from an unidentified source that Tân Sơn Nhứt Airport was surrounded by tanks and troops, likely there might be a coupe or uprising in Saigon. The audience was quite shocked in hearing that. Almost immediately, the priest laughed and said that it was not true; an impending change of regime was good news to those fled the motherland and hoped to return home, similarly was the good news of the New Testament to sinners.

The priest began the first lesson from the Book of Matthew. O how boringly he taught and I learned nothing that evening. We bought a new thick Vietnamese Bible in small print translated almost single-handedly by a priest Nguyễn Thế Thuấn from the original texts. The priest vanished in 1975 being abducted from a bus station in the region of Lâm Đồng. The Bible class was cancelled after only one session due to lack of attendance.

Unknown Church Visitors

A few months later, one Saturday afternoon when I returned home from the weekend job Anna told me that on that morning a group of Vietnamese Protestants, two men and two women knocked at our door for a friendly visit and invited her to attend a Bible study. These people were very friendly and she asked my opinion if she should go, I said it would not hurt at all because our Pope encouraged us to do so. Besides, we could find out if their Bible teaching was more interesting than that of our priest's.

Although I was a new Catholic, I knew all about the follies of the Protestants: they did not believe in the eternal virginity of Mary the Mother of God; preachers wore suits and ties in lieu of priestly attires, could marry and have children. I was convinced that only bachelors and virgins in religious garbs were worthy to serve the holy God. Besides, we have the Pope as the head of Christendom with all the authority, hierarchy and pomp, therefore we were the authentic one and they were estranged rebels.

New Faith

One of the two female visitors came next week and drove Anna and our children to Montrose Baptist Church, a couple miles away. Anna was pleased that the people there were nice and friendly. After learning that I was unable to leave work on Saturday till 3:30 p.m. the Bible study group changed its hour to 4:00 p.m. so that I could join in.

Teacher of the Bible study was Mr. Lê Phước Nguyên (his name means fount of blessings derived from the famous hymn—Come Thou Fount of Every Blessing), a lay preacher from Northern Virginia. The Lê family was among the first believers when the Christian & Missionary Alliance missionaries came to Central Vietnam in the early 1900s. Mr. Nguyên came to the States in the mid-'60s to work for Voice of America. At their spare time, he and his family ministered to the ARVN personnel coming to the MD-VA-DC areas for training, especially the Marines in Quantico.

The class made up of about ten adults. Somehow, I sensed an indescribable peace showed up naturally on Mr. Nguyên and his wife that I had never experienced before in the Catholic churches. The lessons on basic doctrines were simple, straightforward and replete with Bible verses.

In the third or fourth class, during a study break, I approached Mr. Nguyên to talk about a verse listed in the class notes. It was Romans 8:1 "There is therefore now no condemnation to them whom are in Christ Jesus ..." I listened and began to understand the meaning of Christ's death and resurrection for me. The Bible verse was the answer to my "unknowing" pursuit for Truth aroused by the announcement of Vatican.

I lived a life without God, not acknowledging the Creator who made me and kept me mysteriously away from fatal disasters. By the Gospel I was convicted a hell-bound sinner, but by the death of Christ on the cross, God saved me into His kingdom.

"I once was lost but now am found, was blind but now I see."

O what a glorious Savior, what a gracious salvation!

Gradually and slowly line by line, precept by precept, I learned more on the person and work of Christ in the Bible classes and studies through reading and radio.

We were invited to the preacher's home in Northern Virginia for group studies. I was asked to consider baptism and I agreed wholeheartedly.

When I mentioned my wish for baptism to Anna, she vehemently objected. The reason was that she was a fourth-generation Roman Catholic and would not switch to another faith. After some bickering, Anna agreed to see Mr. Nguyên; through his clarification, she also agreed to be baptized!

On one November Sunday afternoon of 1984, the birthday of Anna, the two of us and two others were baptized in a small CMA church in Manassas, Virginia. It was so joyful to share with the congregation in my testimony how truly free I was in comparison to all the other exceptional feelings of walking out of the POW and reeducation camps, landing on the shore of Malaysia, stepping on the soil of the United States for the first time! I praised the Lord for His mercy: He carried me through the turbulence of sicknesses, accidents, war and mishaps, through the valley of the shadow of death. When I was a pagan wanted nothing to do with this foreign Deity, but in mercy the Lord sought and saved His lost sheep.

Pointing me towards the pilgrimage to follow Christ, Mr. Nguyên gave me three important advices:

1. Read the sermons of the late Dr. D. Martyn Lloyd Jones.
2. Stay away from the Scofield Reference Bible.
3. Trust not psychology, psychological counseling, nor psychotherapy.

In all these years these advices provided me godly discernment and understanding. Each time I picked up MLJ's book, the Lord used his preaching to convict me of sin in the presence of the Almighty and then showered me the assurance of salvation perfected by Christ.

Around Christmas 1984, Mr. Nguyên passed an ordination board's assessment and was ordained a minister in Montrose Baptist Church.

The family of Mr. Nguyên had lived in Pleiku in the early 1960's. The watch shop where I picked up my Chinese daily each evening situated next to a pharmacy called Ái Lan, i.e. "love the orchids" turned out to be the one previously operated by Mrs. Nguyên; its original name was Ái Lân or "love thy neighbor".

New Job

Without any involvement on my part, abruptly someone in the workplace I had occasional working contact brought me to another company. The new job offered me a salary as much as my two jobs combined, therefore I could afford to quit the part-time job after four years. Now as a family, we were free to worship on Sunday and take part in church activities on weekends.

The small Vietnamese congregation organized by Pastor Nguyên rented a tiny community center in Northern Virginia, then moved to the chapel of a CMA church worshipping on Sunday afternoons.

New Citizenship

Six months after Anna and I passed the citizenship exam, in September of 1985, the four of us became American citizens. In the swearing-in ceremony in Baltimore, we sat in the back of the hall. We did not see any new citizen representative taking the vow or sing the national anthem or salute the flag. We got in queue to get our certificates and leave without even a paper flag souvenir for such a precious occasion.

Ten years after my citizenship had been stripped away, I was granted citizenship of this great nation on earth, and on this new homeland our Lord put me into His kingdom above.

After two years or so, I told Pastor Nguyên about a dream that I had, in which I was using Cantonese to tell my aunt about the Gospel on the fourth floor terrace of our old home. Strange as it was in the sense that I had until then never read or heard the Word of God in Chinese. Pastor Nguyên advised me that it was the Lord's will for me to return to the Chinese church, I agreed with his idea and encouragement so I started looking for a Chinese church close to home. Finally from a flyer someone stuck in our door handle, I located a Chinese Church in Rockville.

The Chinese Church was much bigger than the Vietnamese CMA Church. After a couple scouting trips we attended the church more frequently. At first we still went to the Vietnamese Church once a month, then because I got involved in the church ministries and our children had suitable Sunday school classes so we settled in the Chinese Church. At first I encouraged Anna to come with us but it was so difficult for her to listen to Cantonese sermons while reading from her Vietnamese Bible, gradually Anna dropped out from the church scene.

Translating Dr. John Sung's Biography

After switching church we still kept in touch with Pastor Nguyên. On one occasion Pastor Nguyên asked about Dr. John Sung the famous Chinese Evangelist during the WWII period. Dr. Sung had come to Vietnam and preached in many cities, the Lord used him to strengthen the Vietnamese churches greatly going through the wars. Pastor Nguyên was saved when he was nine years old when Dr. Sung preached in Đà Nẵng. Pastor Nguyên first wanted to find out was Dr. Sung a MD or a PhD, because the interpreter then did not make the distinctions in Vietnamese. I told him that Sung was a PhD in Chemistry and I had on hand his biography. Pastor Nguyên asked me to translate the life story of Dr. Sung into Vietnamese because the Vietnamese Christians were eager to know more about the Chinese evangelist that had helped the churches in the North under persecution. More than willing I began the project. I translated the book on Dr. Sung onto cassette tapes and mailed to Pastor Nguyên, who had moved to Houston. Pastor Nguyên said that my voice had been known by many Vietnamese Christians not only in the States but also in Eastern Europe for he sent the cassettes to Viet churches throughout the world.

Eventually the book was published in very elegant Vietnamese through the editing of Christian professors. Pastor Nguyên gave me ten copies of the book and I gave them to friends; the one known result was that my buddy Vương Chiêu was blessed by the book which played a role in bringing him and his family to faith. It was so exciting to know that good work honoring our Lord would be used to glorify Him.

Dr. John Sung was one of the three Christians greatly used by the Lord in the beginning of the twentieth century to grow and strengthen the Chinese churches in preparation to face the forthcoming persecution by the Japanese and then the Communist. The other two were Mr. Wang Ming-Dao and Mr. Watchman Nee; all three had no formal theological trainings. Dr. Sung was from a poor pastor's family, he came to study in Ohio Wesleyan University with his substandard English; he got his PhD in five years. Sung became an ecumenical Christian attending the apostate Union Theological Seminary in New York City. After the new birth in Christ he was so zealous to witness in the campus the Seminary locked him up in a mental hospital. Dr. Sung was rescued through legal action by an American missionary after 193 days in the asylum, during the stay there he read the Bible from cover to cover forty times. After the leading of the Lord he returned to China when he was twenty eight, on the way home he threw all his worldly honors such as golden keys for honor citizens of big cities into the Pacific Ocean and brought only his doctoral degree to his disappointed father as a souvenir. Just as exactly as foretold by the Lord that he would serve the Church for fifteen years, Dr. Sung spent those years ministering in the Japanese-occupied China and Southeast Asia. He passed away at age forty four, and Mr. Wang Ming-Dao preached at his funeral.

Chinese Boss

My new employer was an overseas-born Cantonese from Burma, he was one year older than me and his parents originated from the same place as our Dad. He got an MBA after finishing his study in chemistry. He worked very hard, and regularly stayed up till three in the morning to oversee all details of the company. He identified with the patriotic sentiment of overseas Chinese that had been cut off from homeland and despised those Chinese who flattered Westerners.

Once on returning from a family vacation, he told me that he was thinking of me when he was reclining on the beach reading a book about the Vietnam War even though I had not shared with him my past.

On one occasion I wondered if my boss knew the history or origin about a listing of 199 industrial chemicals that the EPA works mentioned all the times; he chuckled and said he made up the list one night in two hours.

He nourished a dream to establish a nation for the overseas Chinese that had been abandoned by the two Chinese governments; so he told me to buy maps of the Andaman Islands in the eastern Indian Ocean as a side project. After my customary quick study I told him that Andaman Islands situated in the path of the yearly cyclones which devastated Bangladesh; it would cost tons of money to buy up the islands to begin with, not to mention developing a sustainable economy and building a self-defense force. That was the end of the project.

Several years after getting to know him, my boss was dying from liver cancer, which was progressed from his boyhood hepatitis. The cancer had already metastasized when it was diagnosed because he did not pay attention to his health until throwing up blood. One day my boss asked me to drive him to Johns Hopkins Hospital. In the cafeteria, he told me that he offered his idea to the hospital lab in purifying the chemotherapy drug to use on him. I asked about his religious belief and he told me that to him Protestantism was objectionable: when he was attending an English-German school in Rangoon where the principal, an ordained minister, was actively involved in politics, therefore he felt more comfortable with the Roman Catholic priests who were well-educated and friendly. He passed away about a month after our talk.

After quitting her job in Holy Cross Hospital Anna also went to work with my previous company and eventually came to work alongside with me in the new firm.

The Pregnancy and Birth of Peter

When William was eleven years old, Anna was pregnant again. Anna worried that she was too old and busy to start over. To prepare for the addition to the family, we found a Vietnamese Obstetrician/Gynecologist in Northern Virginia, Dr. Đặng Phương Thảo.

Seven months into the pregnancy Dr. Thảo ordered a sonogram for Anna, so we went to a clinic in Northern Virginia. Usually the procedure would be performed by a technician and take a few minutes, but after a while the technician asked the radiologist to come to the scene. Anna had to wait an additional ten to fifteen minutes lying down, and it was very hard for her when the bladder was under much pressure at that stage. Afterwards the physician told Anna that he would forward the test result to Dr. Thảo.

A few days went by; one evening when we were having dinner the phone rang. I picked up the phone and Dr. Thảo was on, she told me calmly that the sonogram showed that there were some problems with the baby inside: The baby's head was large and therefore suspicious of having hydrocephalus, it looked like there was a tumor in the baby's belly, and there was at the junction of the umbilical cord with the placenta a small pool of seeping blood. Another sonogram was ordered in case all these were confirmed then she would ask her professors in Georgetown University to perform intrauterine surgery. Haltingly, I gave Anna the bad news; she cried and blamed me having caused this complicated pregnancy.

At the wit's end of man God was our only help; I called Pastor Nguyên in Houston for prayer also the pastor from the Chinese Church. Immediately Pastor Jonathan Liu and Mrs. Liu came. They comforted Anna and encouraged her to trust in the Lord for the baby; they laid hands on her and offered the petition to our Lord.

One week later, another sonogram was performed in Arlington Hospital where Dr. Thảo was affiliated. I stood beside Anna, and the technician just did her job quietly without any comment. The sonogram showed very clearly that it was a boy. We heard nothing from the doctor herself afterwards.

The projected time for delivery of the baby boy was approaching. On the evening of Friday July 13, we did our grocery shopping and Anna showed no sign of discomfort. The next morning, I found trace of blood in the toilet and even though Anna was feeling normal when I raised the question, so for the sake of safety we went to the hospital. When we were there, the signs of birthing came up more conspicuously and Peter was born a couple hours later; weighing seven pounds three ounces, the baby came out normal. When Dr. Thảo was receiving the baby, Anna overheard she talking softly to herself: this was incredible! The not so normal thing was that our baby was born with two incisors on the lower jaw.

After we were back at the patient's room, Anna revealed a secret she had kept to herself for days. On the evening that we asked for prayer from the pastors, at a semi-conscious state in her sleep, Anna looked out to the window and saw brilliantly bright light, at that moment she felt a palm, very hot yet very gentle, rubbed on her belly up and down three times; she broke out in sweat and was awakened from her sleep. In her heart, Anna knew that the hand of the Lord had touched her and healed the baby, but her faith was weak, so she dared not to tell me. When the baby came out Anna was very tense, until she heard the exclamation from the doctor and put it on her stomach. She speedily caressed the baby all over to make sure that it was all right and a miracle did happen!

The Passing of Dad

In the early '60s, Dad got hurt in a car accident on the way to Phnom Penh. The car lost control and hit a tree, and because of that our Father stayed away from learning to drive. After the accident kidney stones began to bother Dad. A Chinese herbalist came to our home many times to take

Dad's pulse and prescribed herbs to clear out the stones. The primary ingredient was the golden coin grass (*Herba lysimachiae*) supposedly could pulverize the stones in the kidney. The herbal medicine was ineffective in this serious case, and Dad switched to Western medicine.

A French physician recommended surgery, but Dad would not take the surgical risk to leave the boys fatherless. Once Dad was in a painful attack of the stones the physician came to make house call and administered morphine. The stones on the X-rays were numerous filling up a kidney. The protein in his urine caked up white rings on the chamber pot that he used at night.

In addition to kidney problems Dad got pemphigus, an immune system related disease, around 1972 and was hospitalized in the Grall Hospital. On his skin were blisters which expanded quickly and merged with surrounding ones to form even bigger ones. It happened during one of my frequent furloughs and I spent an entire day sitting beside his sick bed using needle to prick the blisters and wiped away the liquid with Kleenex. The autoimmune disease was put under control by large dose of steroid.

Dad was very healthy, if not because of his kidney problem his nephrologist swore that he would live to a hundred. After the surgical removal of the diseased kidney in 1980, the remaining healthy kidney function was weakened and finally led to end stage renal disease (ESRD). Since 1994, Dad had to undergo renal dialysis. Before the medical procedure, Dad asked me if he could skip that because he had concerns about this tortuous path to prolong life. It was very difficult for me as a son to give my personal opinion; I did tell him that for his age three years' survival was the average.

By God's grace, I was able to do the least thing for Dad during the ensuing years: Three times a week, at the scheduled time Dad was returning home, I took time off from work, one mile or so away, to help him into a wheelchair from the taxi, and pushed him to the apartment. Three years later, Father passed away due to complication of a dialysis catheter replacement surgery. Around the moment of Father's departure, I got a mysterious vision.

Dad went into a coma a few days after the surgery that replaced yet another clogged catheter, a week or so had gone by and he was transferred from Suburban Hospital in Bethesda to the Mariner's Nursing Home at the other end of Old Georgetown Road. After the hustle and bustle of paper works and Dad was settled in a room; family members were standing around his bed or in the hallway.

We noticed that Father was having problem breathing so we asked a nurse if he could help to ease Dad breathing; and the nurse brought in an aspirator to remove the mucus. Not too long afterwards another nurse came to read the vital signs and she informed us that Dad was at the final moment of his life, quickly the suction tube was removed. Immediately everybody gathered around Dad's bed, I was kind of half-kneeling at the end of the bed.

I had heard and read about the many occasions that all departing souls would always wake up and say goodbye to the loved ones, and this was the first time ever I was to witness death and was not even expecting that our Dad would be able to do that from a coma. A few minutes later, Dad opened his eyes, and someone hushed "He's back!" Dad very serenely, without making any sound, took a look around on all of us around the bed. He closed his eyes and stopped breathing with a light burping noise; some white liquid came down from his nostrils. Before anyone plunged forward to touch Dad, I saw his entire body suddenly appeared as lit-up neon and then the luminescence receded from his feet toward the head, as quick as it appeared the light went away.

When Dad was alive, I had shared with him bits and pieces of the Gospel, but he slighted it gently in the traditional Chinese way that the death of a man was similar to the extinguishing of a candle; if there was a coming judgment, even though he was not perfect, but was not that bad in comparison with so many others. I had invited Dad many times to go to church, but he stayed home in all the seven years that I brought Mom to church. During Dad's coma, I prayed at his bedside and read portions of the Bible to him, hoping that the Lord would have mercy on Dad. Salvation is of the Lord!

For of him, and through him, and to him, are all things: to whom be glory for ever. Amen. Romans 11:36

Farewell to Mom

Mom passed away in January of 2010 after a few visits to the emergency. Mom was ninety two.

Mom grew weaker and weaker after Thanksgiving; she took in only small amounts of fluid and food, the severe constipation causing aches and pains around the abdomen brought her to the emergency time after time.

On January 13, Anna and I took time off before noon to visit Mom at the assisted living in Burtonsville. We picked up Mary on the way so that she could meet grandma yet alive. While we were on the road, I was informed by my brother Ju-Jiang that Mom was waiting for ambulance again. When we arrived at the place, a fire engine was there and a couple firemen were checking on her. Mom was slouching in a wing chair next to the staircase, with her eyes shut and crying pain. Mary tried to pick up Mom's hand but she struggled to pull it out from Mary's grasp. An ambulance came and the crew carried her out on a stretcher. One of the medics asked if we had any preference of hospital, I responded with Holy Cross, which was bigger and convenient to all of us. After contacting the coordinating center, we were told that neither Holy Cross nor Howard General was available and the only choice was Laurel Regional Hospital. We were kind of displeased for it was small and had had bad reports. After obtaining direction from the driver of ambulance we went ahead to get our lunches from McDonald's.

The attending physician in the Emergency Department was from Haiti where a shattering quake that killed thousands occurred just the day before.

Mom was moved to a private room at the second floor. At first an order of no-food-allowed-orally was posted but removed on the second day. A full-liquid diet tray was brought in, it was so much better than those in Holy Cross where Anna and I had worked several years. All our preconceived notion of this hospital had eventually changed and we gave it our highest mark in all aspects.

Mother struggled to take in some food in very minute amount but she could not swallow and she complained about pain in the chest and belly. Her arms were black-and-blue from the I.V. because her veins had shrunk and fluids accumulated around the infusion sites. After talking to the attending staff physician and a social worker we agreed to consider bring Mom to hospice. After a worker from the hospice came to evaluate Mom, we heard nothing about the transfer. Observing that Mother was losing her bodily function, we consulted the physician to stop all IVs and medication and apply comfort-care for a terminal patient. Four days after admitting to the hospital Mom passed away in peace on January 17, 2010, a Sunday. I gave all the praises to our Lord that I was asked by my brothers to pray a farewell prayer by Mom's bedside and performed the internment ceremony of her ashes.

Anna composed a poem in Vietnamese for Mom and I translated it into Chinese and English. The memorial service was held at the same funeral home for Dad. Peter played Amazing Grace with guitar during the memorial and William read the English translation of the poem "Crying Mother dear":

Mother, farewell unto autumns untold
Separation straddles myriad thresholds
To eternity where peace shall reign
No pain nor stupor perchance remain
You fly away from a sapping dream
Awash are we in sad weeping stream
Mother ascend from temporal reach
Fleeting is life as footprints on the beach
We're sending you off, Mom, today
Tears streaking down, murmurs of fate
Mother, calling our gentle Mother!
Countenance dearest blurs behind smother
Gather 'round your serene presence
Final look drinks deep parting cadence.
Goodbye, Mom...

Marriage Certificate

Anna applied for the immigration of her sisters coming to the States since 2000. After the approval from the State Department they waited ten years due to quota and were finally ready to come. Then the Immigration and Customs Enforcement required that Anna had to send them a copy of marriage certificate. My matrimony certificate from the Catholic Church was not considered valid; neither was our common law status in filing joint tax returns for thirty years; nor our immigration approval as couple before leaving Vietnam in 1978; not even our naturalization applications claiming that we were husband and wife. The proposed solution from the agency was that we had to check with the U.S. Embassy in Bangkok Thailand to look up our refugee files when we were in Malaysia. I did check with a church friend in Bangkok working with the Department of Army on HIV vaccine to see if he could help to expedite the process for time was very limited, but it was impossible.

Eventually, the easiest and practical approach was for us to get married officially. So, one day in July of 2010, under the witness of Mary, we were married in the County Courthouse in Rockville. We spent fifty eight dollars to get five copies of the certificate and sent one to Vietnam to complete the process. Again our marriage ceremony was similar to that of our naturalization, no VIPs, no fanfare.

There is one more marriage ceremony we are looking forward to, that is, the wedding feast of the Lamb. There will be joy indescribable in the glory of the Almighty, all our loved ones saved by grace will be present to enjoy the Lord our God forever…

Epilogue

I would like to present in layman terms what I have learned through the years about the humanistic and philosophical teachings which have nothing to do with God at all before my conversion, and for most Asians these are their basis to reject the Bible.

Confucianism: The ideal life is condensed into two words "loyalty" and "forgiveness"; nobody knows about the invisible realm therefore the pragmatic approach of a man is to think and act according to conscience, live a righteous life hence expanding to a perfect family, an idyllic nation, and utopia as the goal of ultimate goodness.

Taoism: All worldly troubles are caused by human contraptions, to ease away all the ills of the society is to follow nature and live simply. We are to snap all the rulers for measuring, break all the scales for weighing, because they result in cheating and inequity; destroy all the legal codes, for when they were laid down loopholes are there for manipulation; do nothing then there is no mistake.

Buddhism: In this life of suffering strive to meditate to arrive at Nirvana which is the end to the perpetual re-incarnations caused by our ignorance. Ultimately all will be free and merge into the Nothingness.

Religions try wholeheartedly to find the answer to the ultimate question of afterlife, but none can; because they know not the cause of all human problems is the sin against God, the Maker and Ruler of heaven and earth.

The only hope for mankind is to trust and obey the Lord and Savior Jesus Christ, the second Person of the triune God who had come into this world, lived a righteous life, died on the cross as a substitute for sinners, was raised from the dead and is alive to rule His creation forever.

> Isaiah 55:1-3 Ho, every one that thirsteth, come ye to the waters, and he that hath no money; come ye, buy, and eat; yea, come, buy wine and milk without money and without price. Wherefore do ye spend money for *that which is* not bread? and your labour for *that which* satisfieth not? hearken diligently unto me, and eat ye *that which is* good, and let your soul delight itself in fatness. Incline your ear, and come unto me: hear, and your soul shall live; and I will make an everlasting covenant with you, *even* the sure mercies of David.
>
> Isaiah 55:6-9 Seek ye the LORD while he may be found, call ye upon him while he is near: Let the wicked forsake his way, and the unrighteous man his thoughts: and let him return unto the LORD, and he will have mercy upon him; and to our God, for he will abundantly pardon. For my thoughts *are* not your thoughts, neither *are* your ways my ways, saith the LORD.
>
> John 14:6 Jesus saith unto him, I am the way, the truth, and the life: no man cometh unto the Father, but by me.

Amen!

About the Author

David Tran served six years in the Army of the Republic of Vietnam, spent three years in POW and concentration camps, survived two boat trips and struggled six months in the Malaysian refugee camps. He resettled to America in 1979, redeemed by Christ in 1984, and retired in 2015. Anna and David have been blessed with a forty one year marriage, one daughter, two sons, and four grandchildren.

CPSIA information can be obtained
at www.ICGtesting.com
Printed in the USA
LVHW112013200120
644177LV00005B/409